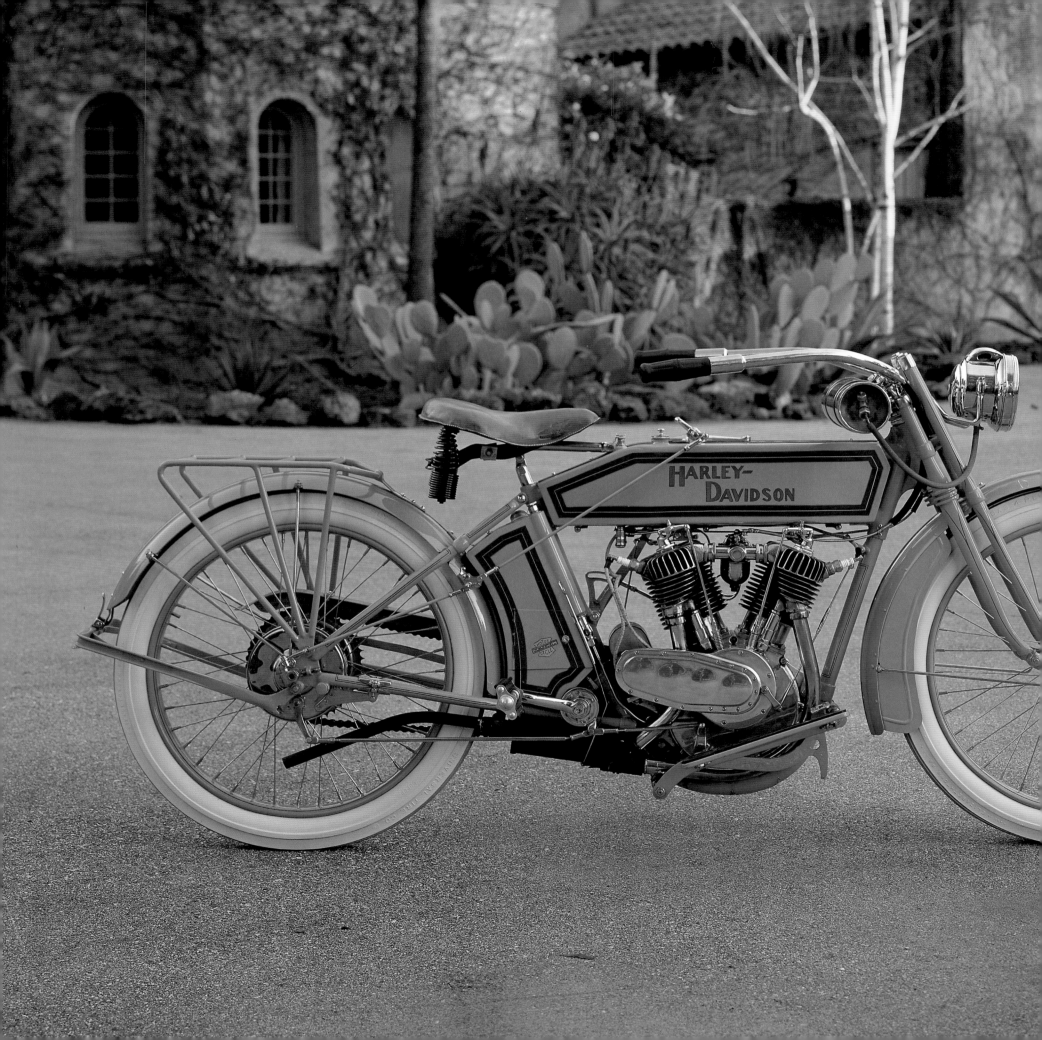

Classic
MOTORCYCLES

Mark Gardiner

MetroBooks

MetroBooks

An Imprint of Friedman/Fairfax Publishers

Library of Congress Cataloging-in-Publication Data available upon request.

ISBN 1-56799-460-1

Editor: Tony Burgess
Designer: Robbi Firestone
Photography Editor: Kathryn Culley
Production Manager: Camille Lee

Color separations by Ocean Graphic International Company Ltd.
Printed in China by Leefung-Asco Printers Ltd.

10 9 8 7 6 5 4 3 2 1

For bulk purchases and special sales, please contact:
Friedman/Fairfax Publishers
Attention: Sales Department
230 Fifth Avenue
New York, NY 10001
212/685-6610 FAX 212/685-3916

Visit our website:
www.metrobooks.com

Dedication

This book is dedicated to clubmen everywhere.

Acknowledgments

This book is a personal interpretation of motorcycle history. It reflects the experiences and opinions of motorcyclists, racers, mechanics, historians, and writers too numerous to mention. Some, however, contributed too much to ignore. *The Complete Illustrated Encyclopedia of the World's Motorcycles*, a book by the late Erwin Tragatsch, served as a basic reference for things like dates and names; Hugo Wilson's *The Ultimate Motorcycle Book* was used in a similar capacity; and back issues of the excellent magazines *Fast Classics* and *Classic Bike* were dog-eared by my research. The Reynolds-Alberta Museum's exhibit *Forever Motorcycles* in Wetaskiwin, Alberta, and the Trev Deeley Motorcycle Museum in Richmond, British Columbia, provided me with opportunities to see many classic machines I would otherwise have known only from photos.

No writer is any better than his editors. My sister, Diana Gardiner, provided a very thorough review of the manuscript. Thanks to her, Tony Burgess, my editor at the Michael Friedman Publishing Group, may not realize just how meager my writing skills really are!

Last but not least, I must thank vintage racer, artist, and social historian Bill Rodgers. Bill provided reference material, a critical review of early drafts, and many penetrating insights. If, as a reader, you catch an error, it can be chalked up to me. But if you find yourself thinking, "Wow, I never realized that!" there's a good chance the observation came from Bill.

TABLE OF CONTENTS

Foreword

Cycle World magazine ruined my life. In 1970, upon my return from a stint in the Peace Corps, a diabolical friend loaned me a bound collection of the infamous magazine. The April 1962 issue had a road test and engine analysis of the Matchless G-50 CSR Golden Eagle. Overhead cams. Hand-polished rocker arms. Big bore, short stroke. Magnesium sand castings. Vernier timing sprockets. I swooned at the thought of holding these magical parts in my hands. It was love at first sight.

I had to have one. Law school intervened. None were to be found. The search continued. Dick Mann's G-50 appeared, in bits. Al Gunter's bike was next. An AJS 7R from Jim Cotherman. A G-50 from Bob Hansen. Tony Woodman's. Don Vesco's. Help and bits arrived from Paddy Driver, Ray Cowles, Tom Arter. The first of four "triple-knockers" (7R3A) came from Steve Griffith. Big pieces came from Alan Latham, Eric Biddle, George Beale. The attitude was always "Buy it now, figure out how to pay for it later."

Team Obsolete was born. We went racing with these wonderful machines before it was in vogue to do so, or even to collect them. We won more than one hundred races worldwide. We sponsored many happy riders. We never stopped. We still do it.

The G-50s and 7Rs brought us to the fabled venues of the world: Daytona, Laguna Seca, Mosport, Brands Hatch, Mallory Park, Dundrod, Misano, Monthlerey, Assen, Circuit Paul Ricard, Pukekohe, Bathhurst, Tsuba (Tokyo), La Carrera. Most special was the Isle of Man, where Dave Roper set two lap records and won a TT, a Tourist Trophy, the only American to do so, ever.

Motorcycles are the ultimate expression of motorized passion. Those from the past, those that predate CAD-CAM design and robotic construction, those that were built in tiny "factories" by hand, are the pure expression of their makers' passion.

We who celebrate the rich history of classic motorcycles keep that passion alive. For some, it is classic street bikes, for others, pre-1965 Moto Cross, or Classic Observed Trials machines. There seems to be room for everyone. For Team Obsolete it has been a crazy roller coaster ride, a mixture of camaraderie, late nights, good friends, worn out motors, knowing smiles, tolerant families, and seductively beautiful bikes.

For two decades I have tried to read almost everything published on the subject of classic motorcycles. Mark Gardiner's book is perhaps a new high-water mark, because of his ability to clarify the complexities of the subject and to put it into perspective. With its breadth, this book has prompted me to recall that classic motorcycles are different things to different people, and that each of us was introduced to the sport for different reasons, under different circumstances. For me, it was *Cycle World* magazine.

In the words of Jerry Garcia, "What a long, strange trip it's been..."

Rob Iannucci, Team Obsolete

Brooklyn Heights, New York

Author's Preface

I remember the first motorcycle race I ever saw. It was in the sixties in France. In my memory, I want it to have been the French Grand Prix, but it might have been any club race. There were posters up in a nearby town announcing *Courses à Motos*. I begged my parents to take me.

It was hot, probably August. The track was laid out in a forest, and we watched from the shade of the trees. We couldn't see the grid, but in the distance, we heard each start, from the insane shriek of the 50cc Kriedlers to the flat staccato of the Norton 500s. Each sound would build, then doppler down an octave as the pack flashed past, disappearing back into the sun-dappled forest.

Those riders, clad in black leather and pudding-bowl helmets, still ride through my memory, and thirty years later, I still chase them on my own RZ 350.

Motorcycles have existed for about one hundred years. Over that time, it is safe to say that few inventions have captured the imagination of so many people. Is it the exposed engines? The visceral sense of wind-buffeted speed? With motorcycles' far lighter mass, riders have always enjoyed acceleration, stopping, and handling that few car-bound drivers understand. But there's more to it than that—such as a sense of freedom and an opportunity for self-expression that most possessions do not offer.

To research the history of motorcycles is to be awed by the insights of the engineers, dazzled by the brilliance of designers, humbled by the bravery of racers, and, yes, baffled by blundering businessmen. I have tried to tell the human story of motorcycling through its machines. There is not nearly enough space in this book to cover every motorcycle worthy of the title "classic." Nor do I pretend to have such encyclopedic knowledge. To the fans of motorcycles that are underrepresented or overlooked in these pages, I offer apologies. Rest assured that I, too, realize there are marques worthy of books all their own that have gone unmentioned in *Classic Motorcycles*.

Many readers, I know, will highlight errors or pinpoint omissions in the text and captions. For the sake of future editions, I hope that, instead of scorning the author, they will note opportunities for improvement and forward them to me through the publisher.

Introduction

What makes a classic motorcycle? Well, for one thing, it isn't modern.

If it's old enough, or rare enough, a motorcycle that was once merely "used" may earn the title "classic" just for having survived. The chronology of motorcycle development is complex. There are evolutionary paths that start before their time, die off, and reappear later somewhere else. Fascinating marques rise and fall. Characters who revolutionized the industry fade into history. Fans of a particular marque or period define "classic" from their own unique perspectives. But for all that, it is possible to look at the history of the industry as a whole and agree on its natural breakdown into several broad periods.

The first of these is the Pioneer era, lasting from the invention of motorcycles to World War I. The origins of the motorcycle, originally just a bicycle with a small motor attached, are still very evident in surviving Pioneer bikes. Any motorcycle in running condition from this period is virtually a museum piece, and it is unlikely that many restorable ones are still awaiting discovery.

The Vintage era corresponds to the period from 1920 to the end of World War II. This was a period of great innovation in which motorcycles moved beyond their bicycle roots to assume surprisingly modern shapes and performance. Working motorcycles from this period are still rare and valuable, though a few are put on the road by Vintage buffs. Rare is the lover of these machines who does not dream of a ray of light in some dusty garage, catching the gleam of a Harley Knucklehead, unridden since an old uncle went off to war. Now, unfortunately, such machines are found only in daydreams, no longer in real barns.

The Classic period extends roughly from 1945 to 1975. This was a time less of revolution than of evolution. Virtually every feature that defines these motorcycles made its initial appearance in the Vintage period or even earlier. These included stiff frames with telescopic forks, rear swing arms, and hydraulic damping for improved handling. The control layout of foot-operated rear brake and gearshift, hand-operated clutch and front brake, and a twist-grip throttle became standard. Taken together, these features make classic motorcycles easy for the modern rider to get used to.

Unlike cars or planes of historical interest, classic motorcycles can still be owned by hobbyists of average means, and thousands of these machines still see regular use. There are too many motorcycles to include them all in this text, and the group here is simply a matter of personal taste. The motorcycles selected have been chosen, first and foremost, for elegance and appropriateness to their task. Models that introduced significant technical features are favored, as are those that covered themselves with glory on the racetrack. Some serve to illustrate a particular historical point. While equally worthy ones have gone unmentioned, any of the motorcycles selected could be a collector's pride.

When does the Classic period end? The motorcycles described as "classic" in this book all appeared prior to 1975. Although this date is a matter of editorial convenience, I have defined the end of the Classic period by the onset of a series of technical advances. Among these features are disc brakes, cast wheels, rear monoshocks, water cooling, and alloy "deltabox"-style frames in which the engine functions as a stressed member.

Each of these developments made intermittent appearances earlier in history, but at some point between the mid-seventies and the mid-eighties, they stopped being novelties and came to be expected by the motorcycle-buying public. Fashions come and go; only time will tell which of the bikes that offer such "post-Classic" features will end up being sought by collectors.

Chapter

1

Pioneers

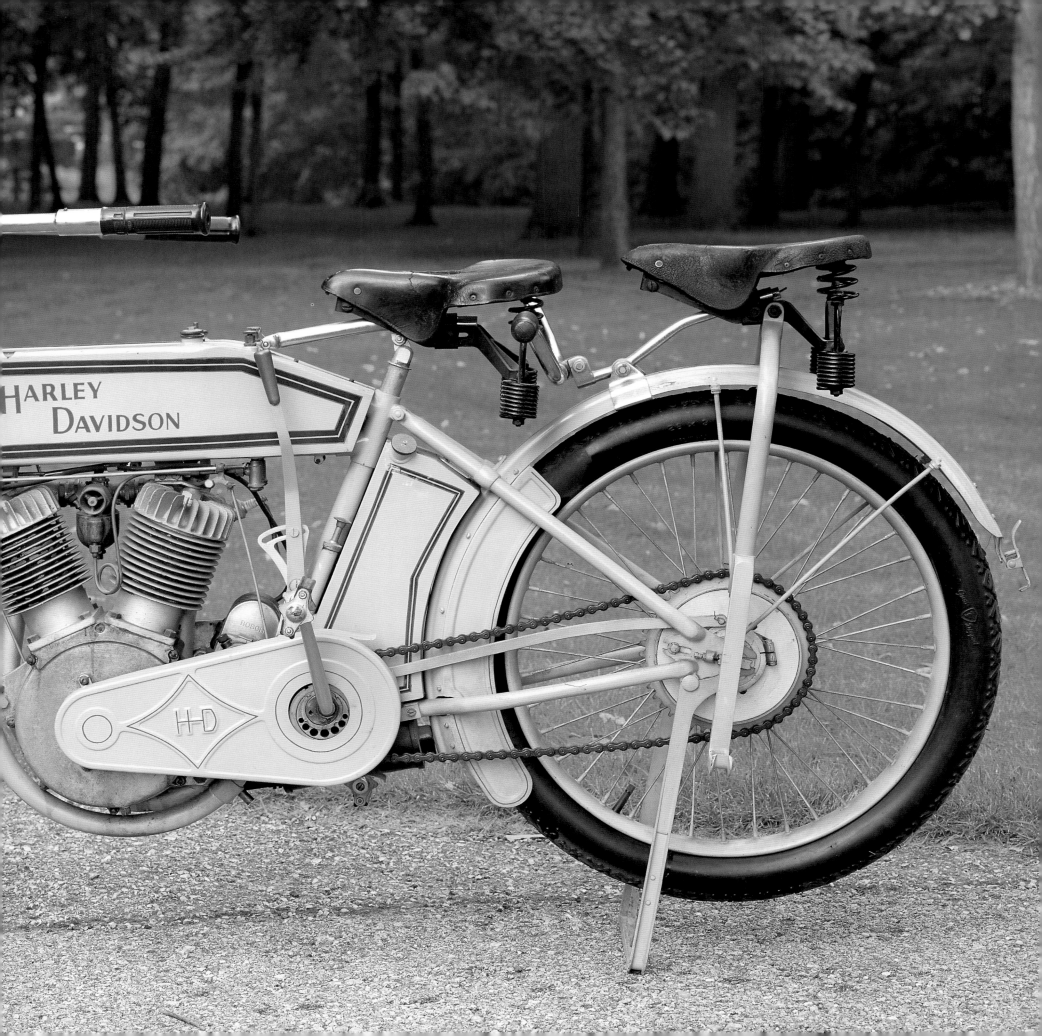

he first documented "motorcycle" was built by Gottlieb Daimler and Wilhelm Maybach in 1885. It was made mostly of wood, with large wheels fore and aft, and smaller stabilizer wheels to the sides. As jarring as the metal-shod wooden wheels must have been on the unpaved roads of the time, Daimler's son, Paul, managed to ride the contraption about 3.1 miles (5km), from their workshop in Cannstatt to Unterturkheim and back.

Hildebrand and Wolfmuller, in Munich, were the first to offer a motorcycle for commercial sale. Their device was a two-cylinder design, with the connecting rods attached directly to the rear wheel. Curiously, they chose not to have the rear wheel act as a flywheel, but rather used elastic rubber straps to return the piston for the next firing stroke.

While these earliest motorcycles remain historical curiosities, neither is really the ancestor of the modern motorcycle. After all, a variety of internal and external combustion engines had existed for decades, and primitive bicycles— "velocipedes," without pedals or steering—had been used as toys for hundreds of years. For a true motorcycle to begin evolving, two things had to happen, and conditions would not be quite right for another few years.

The first condition was the rise of the bicycle in its modern form. This was the Rover Safety Bicycle, which made use of the still-current "diamond" frame, steering head, pedals connected to the rear wheel by a roller chain, and two wheels of moderate size. The Rover made riding a bicycle safe and easy. Three years later, a Belfast veterinarian, J.B. Dunlop, patented the pneumatic tire. After that, bikes lost their nickname of "bone shakers."

The second condition for a true motorcycle to begin evolving was the development of a sufficiently small and powerful gas-powered internal combustion engine. This was achieved by Count Albert de Dion and Georges Bouton in the mid-1890s. Over the next ten years, thousands of de Dion–Bouton engines were built under license and

Pages 14-15: **One of the "Silent Grey Fellows" from Milwaukee. This c. 1915 Harley Davidson made about 11 horsepower.** *Opposite, top:* **The first commercially sold motorcycle, by Hildebrand & Wolfmuller, 1896.** *Opposite, bottom:* **1903 Bouchet, with a de Dion engine. Note that chain drive from pedals and belt drive from engine are independent.** *Above:* **Purposeful-looking 1911 Indian with racing handlebars. The trademark trailing-link leaf-spring forks are already standard. Indian won the Isle of Man Senior TT in this year.** *Right:* **De Dion engines were fitted to a variety of vehicles, including this fin-de-siècle tricycle and trailer.**

attached to bicycles. The first manufacturers were concentrated primarily in France and Belgium, but builders were soon at work across the continent, in Britain, and in the New World.

It is safe to say that, of all the motorcycle brands that have ever existed, most flourished and died out in this earliest period. In hundreds of tiny ateliers and backyard sheds, tinkerers and inventors cobbled together bikes of which there are now no records at all. The few bikes that do exist are museum pieces; they offer none of the conve-

niences deemed essential by modern motorcyclists, such as brakes, gears, clutches, or throttles.

These features were not immediately missed at the turn of the century, and motorcycles already seemed to be capturing the imagination in ways other machines did not. Sales were brisk and encouraged builders to improve performance, safety, comfort, and practicality. Before long, motorcycles were much faster than bicycles and nearly as reliable.

One of the first North American builders was Oscar Hedstrom, a gifted bicycle mechanic from Springfield, Massachusetts. At the turn of the century, board-track bicycle racing was a popular spectator sport. Hedstrom set out to build a motorized pacer bike, which would allow a bicycling coach to keep up with his athletes. He adapted a de Dion design with a carburetor of his own invention, and the result was so successful that George W.

Hendee, a local industrialist, put him on his payroll. They chose the name "Indian" as their trademark.

In 1906, the Indian was typical of other motorcycles in that it lacked a clutch and thus still needed to be stalled at every stop. The bicycle's chain drive survived intact on the right side of the machine, while the completely independent motor belt drive was mounted on the left. Indians were among the first motorcycles to be equipped with

Pioneers

While at least seventy-five U.S. manufacturers built motorcycles around 1910, only a handful survived beyond the stock market collapse of 1929. Harley-Davidson and Indian were sufficiently robust. So was the Excelsior Supply and Manufacturing Co. of Chicago.

Amazingly, the Chicago manufacturer was one of four companies marketing motorcycles under the name Excelsior in the twenties. As such, the American company was prevented from exporting its motorcycles to Britain as "Excelsiors" by a British firm that was building bikes of the same name in Birmingham.

The American Excelsiors were sold in England as "American X" and "Super X" V-twins, along with the in-line four-cylinder design designed by Bill Henderson, produced under license, and marketed simply as a Henderson. In turn, the British Excelsiors were prevented from selling their motorcycles under that trademark in Germany—where two firms were building their own Excelsiors!

This name game was further complicated by the fact that, after selling the rights to his in-line four to Excelsior, Henderson continued to produce a very similar motorcycle under the new name Ace. In 1927, Indian acquired the assets of Ace, and Henderson's design was sold under its final guise, the Indian 4, for many years.

In 1919, Harley-Davidson's sales reached nearly thirty thousand units but collapsed to ten thousand the following year, as the full effect of mass production and sales on credit pulled families out of the motorcycle market and put them into Model Ts. Like any modern enterprise, H-D pared back to its core business. In Harley's case, this dictated selling off its bicycle division. After the Depression, the president of Excelsior did the same thing. The Chicago manufacturer abandoned motorcycles to focus on his traditional family business of bicycles. His family name? Schwinn.

But what became of the other American brands? Many tinkerers and bicycle mechanics threw in the rag around 1912 as motorcycles became increasingly complex and expensive;

Opposite, top: **An enduring symbol of the Depression, a family ruined by the Dustbowl pauses in their westward trek.** *Opposite, bottom:* **By the time that New Deal road building was complete, only a handful of motorcycle manufacturers remained.** *Above:* **A 1914 Excelsior, on the eve of Britain's entry into the Great War.**

customers began to expect features like clutches and gearboxes when they had earlier accepted machines without even such niceties as a throttle!

A few years later, many small shops converted to war production. After the Armistice, they realized that Henry Ford was able to offer a Model T for the price of a sidecar rig and that the motorcycle's role as a form of basic transportation was over.

By the twenties, about a dozen brands—mostly quality machines—survived. Then, as now, motorcycles were discretionary purchases, and with the onset of the Dust Bowl years, sales dried up. During the New Deal, thousands of miles of highway were built as make-work projects, but by then virtually the only American-made motorcycles you could ride on them were Harley-Davidsons and Indians.

This era produced many brands that have since vanished from America. The Apache, a 600cc single-cylinder made by Brown and Beck in Denver, Colorado, went out of production in 1911. It was actually some years before Denver was connected to the outside world by anything remotely resembling a road. The Armac was made by Archie McCullen in St. Paul, Minnesota, until 1913 and was one of several early designs to channel the engine exhaust through one of the frame tubes. Bayley-Flyers were produced immediately prior to World War I, and offered several intriguing features, such as a shaft drive and a type of "automatic" transmission. Cyclone, at the same time, raced another design that was far ahead of its time: the first 1,000cc V-twin equipped with overhead camshafts.

Even then, Americans had little interest in lightweight motorcycles. The Evans factory built an elegant little 119cc two-stroke in the early twenties, which was licensed to Stock of Germany.

A great trademark isn't everything, and thus the Flying Merkel company was active only until 1915. The machines were bright yellow, and were among the first to introduce two-speed transmissions and an electric starter.

Iver-Johnson, like BSA (Birmingham Small Arms), FN (Fabrique Nationale), and Enfield, produced both motorcycles and guns. Iver-Johnson's motorcycles were better than their firearms, but in 1915 they stopped producing bikes and targeted the arms market.

Perhaps the most interesting response to competition from car manufacturers was the Neracar scooter, almost eponymously named by its designer, J. Neracher. Neracher set out to create a motorcycle that was nearly a car. Neracars, produced during the twenties, were excellent but highly unorthodox vehicles resembling a long, low step-through scooter. An ingenious front suspension layout predated the Yamaha GTS by seventy years.

Schickels were produced between 1912 and 1915. They were noteworthy for their (cast!) alloy frames with integral gas tank. Reading-Standard had been one of America's leading motorcycle brands throughout the Pioneer era, but succumbed to market forces in 1922. Like Ace, Reading-Standard was a solidly established second-tier brand, just below Harleys, Indians, and Excelsiors. Most R-S motorcycles were old reliable side-valve designs, but works racers were given more advanced machines with overhead cams.

Left: **Reading Standard motorcycles were particularly popular in the American West. The factory-built tuned racing models were among the first to be equipped with chain drives, in 1902, but "production" models relied on belt drives until much later.** *Below:* **The Merkel (later "Flying Merkel") company produced big motorcycles only until 1915. A limited number of small mopeds, such as this one, continued to be produced for some years.** *Opposite:* **1916 Thor. The Aurora Manufacturing Co. stopped building motorcycles when America entered World War I. After the Armistice, the company produced only home appliances.**

could be removed for servicing while leaving the bicycle in riding condition!

Indian remained interested in the board tracks, which were soon the venues for races between pacer bikes. At first, production models were raced, but by the early 1910s manufacturers realized the value of winning races in front of crowds of ten thousand or more. The manufacturers began building ever-faster works bikes, which were supplied to riders competing against entries from Merkel, Excelsior, and Thor.

twist grips; both grips twisted, with one controlling the throttle and the other the spark advance. The 17-cubic-inch engine operated on a total loss lubrication system and generated 2 horsepower.

Although the Indian had a head start, by the time this model had reached the market, archrival Harley-Davidson was entering their first year of real production, building fifty 3-horsepower singles. The Armac, built in St. Paul, Minnesota, was also similar but made innovative use of the frame tubing to route the engine exhaust down and back.

Although heavy, these "motorcycles" were still bicycles equipped with motors. Those built by Canada Cycle and Motor (CCM) were powered by a 1.5-horsepower unit imported from Motosacoche a Geneve—very high-quality power plants that were, literally, built like a Swiss watch. CCM mounted the engine with seven clips so that it

Pioneers

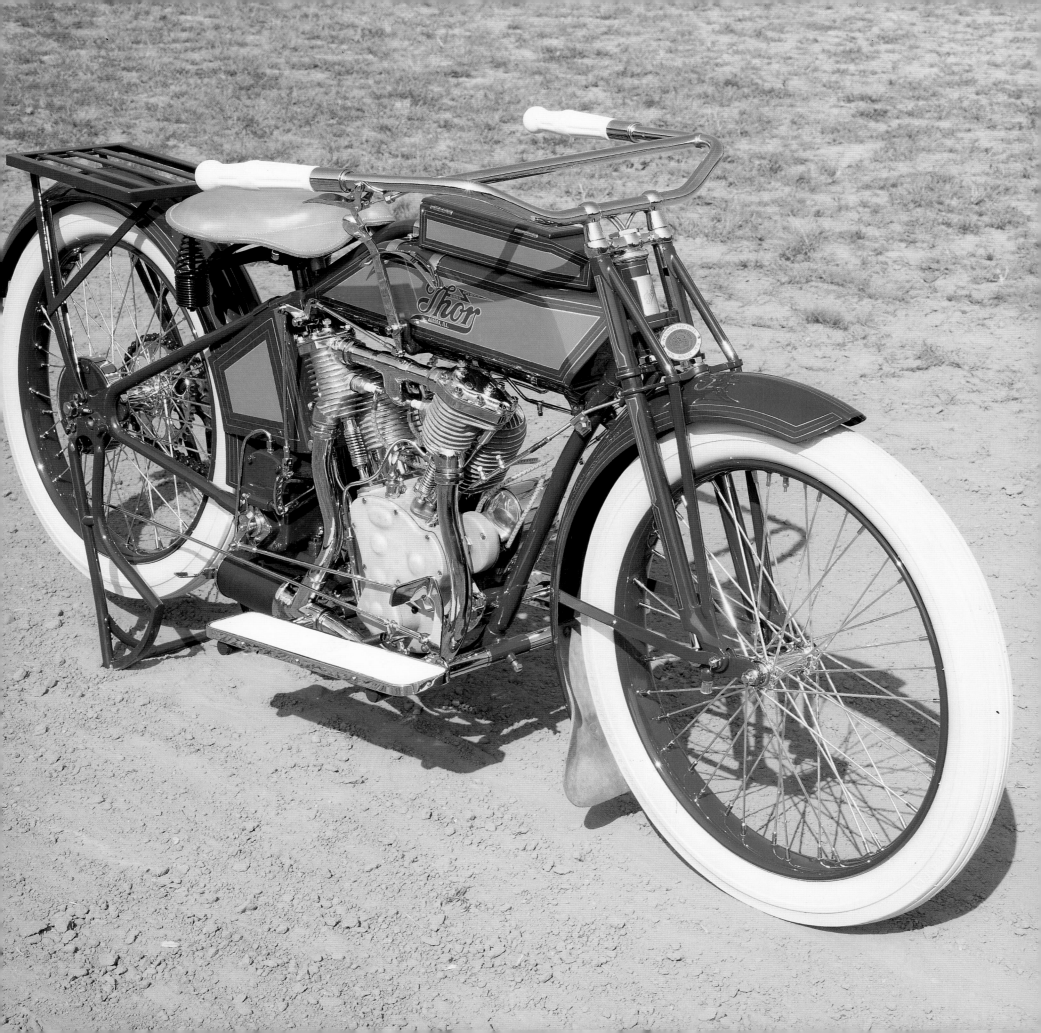

The bicycle tracks were too small for motorcycles, which by 1910 were already reaching speeds of 100 miles per hour (161kph). Jack Prince, a promoter of board-track races, built a chain of tracks across the country. Starting in Los Angeles, he constructed the quarter-mile (402m) Coliseum, and in the next three years built a dozen more, each up to 2 miles (3.2km) in length. Corners were gently banked on the superspeedways, but were nearly vertical in the half-mile (804m) and smaller "soup bowls."

Prince's races were spectacular, but he had little concern for the safety of riders or, for that matter, of his fans. Horrific crashes were common, as the bikes of the period dropped lots of oil onto the track surface. After seven fans and riders were killed in a single crash in Newark, New Jersey, in 1912, the leading manufacturers agreed to withdraw from board-track racing. Factory-supported riders on works bikes were not seen for most of the next year. In 1913, the Federation of American Motorcyclists (FAM) decided that the national championship races would be contested on the less profitable, but far safer, dirt tracks.

Perhaps the ultimate weapon for board or dirt tracks at the time was the Indian Model H racer of 1916. Indian's characteristic V-twin was specially equipped with four-valve-per-cylinder heads, whose exposed rocker arms and springs gave the motorcycle a menacing, businesslike air. While street bikes of the time already had some suspension, the undamped springs contributed to comfort at the expense of handling. Thus, the Model

H is completely unsprung for the lowest possible center of gravity.

According to FAM rules, a specified number of eight-valvers had to be sold in order for the factory to race the design, but in reality this model was a full works machine, intentionally priced beyond the reach of most privateers. Its outrageous cost? $350.

Even before World War I, the American racing scene was dominated by the ovals, while European racing took place on roads. The first motorcycle Tourist Trophy races took place on the Isle of Man in 1907, and within a few years, the TT had become the most important racing event in Europe. "The Indians Are Coming!" trumpeted the British press in 1911 as the powerful, reliable American machines arrived to compete. That year, they dominated the Senior TT, taking first, second, and third.

However, in 1912 (and again in 1913), the Indians were defeated by Scott motorcycles. These were designed by Alfred Angus Scott. He was the most iconoclastic motorcycle designer who ever lived, the holder of more than sixty patents, and one of the first people to build a motorcycle frame not based on that of a bicycle. He was quick to adopt kick starters and chain drive, and among the first to include a two-speed gearbox. He favored small two-stroke twins, which he water-cooled. Scott's engines eerily predicted those seen seventy years later in motorcycles such as Yamaha's club racer RZ 350.

Opposite, top: **Board-track racers drafting on the near-vertical banking of the Baltimore and Washington Speedway, c.1916.** *Opposite, bottom:* **1929 Scott Super Squirrel. Even without Scott at the helm, the company continued to produce motorcycles that bristled with innovations. This 596cc 2-stroke was water cooled, and good for 80 mph (129kph).** *Above:* **The motorcycle is as idiosyncratic as its rider: "Cannonball" Baker rode this Neracar from New York to Los Angeles on only 45 gallons (170L) of fuel, laying claim to the transcontinental economy record. Note unique front suspension layout.**

Not to be outdone, Indian introduced the Hendee Special in 1914, claiming (with some justification) that it was the most advanced design ever. This model was the first to offer a functional electric start and an electric headlamp. The 61-cubic-inch V-twin, with hand-operated clutch and two-speed transmission, propelled the Special to 55 miles per hour (88.5kph). It featured a trailing link front, leaf-spring suspension, and a leaf-spring rear swing arm. The passenger seat had its own elaborate spring mounting. "Cannonball" Baker became a national celebrity when he used a Special to travel from California to New York in the record time of eleven days, twelve hours, and ten minutes. While Indian would produce motorcycles for another thirty years, business prospects would never be brighter.

World War I was a watershed for the American motorcycle industry. During the war, all combatants made extensive use of motorcycles, mainly for dispatch riders. Many major manufacturers devoted anywhere from half to 100 percent of their production to the war effort. Other builders retooled, putting their skilled metalworkers to work making aircraft engines, guns, etc.

By the time the war was over, the American motorcycle business had already been changed forever by Henry Ford's two great inventions: the assembly line and automotive financing. Economies of scale made it possible for Ford to sell his characterless Model T for little more than a typical motorcycle, effectively taking the "basic transportation" market away from motorcycle manufacturers. The demographic group of adventurous young men who might have chosen a motorcycle in spite of the availability of cheap cars was decimated in WWI.

The handful of surviving American producers retrenched, and America lost much of its momentum as an innovator in motorcycle design and engineering. European motorcycle makers were not faced with a similar challenge until after the next war, when the unprepossessing Morris Minor dealt its body blow to the mighty British marques.

23

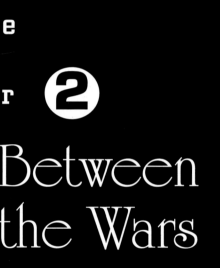

Between the Wars

etween the Great War and the next war, the die was cast for the future of motorcycling. In America, these were challenging times to be a motorcycle manufacturer, but it was a golden age in Europe, especially in Great Britain.

European car manufacturers had not fully embraced mass production, so cars weren't yet affordable to the working man. This, combined with shorter average travel distances, crowded cities with cramped streets, and a (slightly) more temperate climate, made motorcycles a logical choice for basic transportation. Tourist Trophy and Grand Prix styles of road racing thrived; more than American ovals, they encouraged the development of superior technology for road-going machines.

Massive government war-material programs had enabled manufacturers to buy new equipment. Triumph alone supplied more than thirty thousand motorcycles to Allied forces (despite the fact that the company was founded by a pair of German expatriates). Soldiers returning from the front had seen for themselves just how practical these machines had become.

This was the last chance for individual entrepreneurs and engineers to set up shop, and during the 1920s literally hundreds of marques were available to the British buyer. Most of these brands deservedly disappeared, but there were still dozens of factories building really good machines that were capable of holding their own in races and were more practical and safer than ever on the streets.

Of the new motorcycles, none was better than the Brough Superior. George Brough had been working for his father's motorcycle company that they called, simply, Brough. The senior Brough's steadfast reliance on a comparatively old-fash-

Pages 24–25: **This 1000cc JAP-engined Brough Superior laid claim to the Brooklands track record, c.1925. George Brough himself was often the rider on such record attempts.** *Left:* **Sunbeam from 1920. (See p. 30)** *Above:* **"The war to end all wars;" a British soldier's side-hack in Egypt.** *Below:* **The next war: Canadian Army dispatch riders were first trained at Camp Borden, in Ontario. Here riders on a Harley and Norton 16H practice a ford.** *Opposite:* **1920 ABC. While it was in many respects a technologically advanced motorcycle, warranty problems contributed to the collapse of the manufacturer, Sopwith.**

ioned flat-twin engine frustrated George, who struck out on his own, determined to build the very best machines.

Brough Superiors were most commonly built with V-twin engines supplied by James A. Prestwich (the famous JAP customer engines), although Matchless and superb MAG power plants were also used. Customer engines were often supplied to George in special tunings, allowing him to guarantee that his SS100 was in fact capable of reaching 100 miles per hour (161kph). Most of George's customers ordered directly from the factory, so each of these custom-made machines fit its owner like a tailored suit.

George licensed the springer fork used by Harley-Davidson and mated it to a chassis with the Bentley and Draper swing arm, putting the spring under the seat; it was a rear suspension layout that would be seen on Grand Prix racers in the seventies. Suspension was not the only area in which George Brough was an innovator; nestled between the cylinders was a unique single carburetor with two float bowls.

George's motorcycles were also beautifully styled, finished, and assembled. *The Motorcyclist*, a magazine of the day, called them "the Rolls-Royce of motorcycles." George wanted to use this claim in his marketing efforts, and was permitted to do so after Rolls-Royce had examined one of his machines and, surprisingly, concurred with *The Motorcyclist*'s assessment.

George Brough's best-known customer was T.E. Lawrence, then already famous as Lawrence of Arabia. Now shrouded in Brough Superior legend, Lawrence was said to have five (or was it six, or seven?) of the machines. It is not clear whether he owned them consecutively or concurrently. He called each one "George," it is also reported, after his friend George Bernard Shaw. Or he called them "Boanerges," after the fire gods of Norse legend. It is indubitably true that Lawrence was killed in a crash on one of his beloved Superiors in 1935.

In recent years (as the price of Brough Superiors has pierced the $100,000 mark), criticism has been voiced that George Brough was not a particularly skilled engineer or designer. Some point out that his motorcycles were largely assembled from brought-in pieces: customer engines, gearboxes by Sturmey-Archer, Lucas electrics, etc. This view doesn't do justice to the elegance with which those elements were combined.

During World War I, Rolls-Royce was so impressed with George's craftsmanship that his factory was used to manufacture the crankshafts of Merlin aircraft engines (which powered Hurricane fighters). After the war, Brough wanted to resume motorcycle production, but gave up when he could not find an adequate supply of engines.

Meanwhile, back in America, Hendee and Hedstrom had been forced to give up control of Indian to investors in exchange for capital. As minority shareholders, the pair quit the board of directors. While Indian foundered in the twenties, it still managed to release the Scout and, in 1928, the brilliant Model 101 Scout.

management was loathe to leave well enough alone, and in 1932 the Model 101 was replaced with a machine that inserted the Scout's 600cc engine into the much larger Chief frame. While this eliminated the cost of building two frames, the new Scouts were underpowered and clumsy. With only four years of production, 101 Scouts are now among the most sought-after motorcycles.

Harley-Davidson had also looked at America and realized that cars had become the utilitarian choice for transportation. While the overall motorcycle market was shrinking, there remained the "sport riders" of the day—gentlemen interested in riding for pleasure. Harley had been making the twin-cam FH motor for hillclimb competitions since 1924. In 1928, they released a pair of twin-cam "sports" models, the JH (1000cc) and the 1200cc JDH.

These were Harley's top-of-the-line street machines, equipped with twin headlights and, for the first time, a front brake. The extra stopping power must have been welcome, as the JDH was among the fastest production motorcycles of its day, with a top speed of more than 100 miles per

Pages 28–29: **1938 Indian 4. This engine, which produced about 40 horsepower, was licensed by the designer, Bill Henderson, to Excelsior, Ace, and finally Indian.** *Above:* **What a difference a decade makes. In 1920 Sunbeam won the Senior TT. This 1920 Sunbeam, while not a racer, is quite different than the overhead cam Norton seen to the right, which would have been typical of TT competitors by 1928. Note the inadequate "dummy belt drive" front brake on the road-going Sunbeam.** *Below:* **Hillclimbing was a uniquely American sport. During the Depression, it was popular because of the low cost to event promoters.** *Opposite, top:* **1928 Norton CS1. 490cc. On a machine similar to this, Stanley Woods would have been capable of a 60 mph (106.4kph) average lap of the Isle of Man "Mountain" circuit.** *Opposite, bottom:* **Harley racer, 1920.**

The 101, designed by Charles Franklin, is widely recognized as the best Indian of them all. It was powered by a compact, side-valve 600cc V-twin engine, which was mounted in a long, low chassis. Indian's standard leaf-spring front suspension doesn't seem as modern as the girder forks that were being used on the sporty European bikes of the day, but the 101 was immediately recognized for its combination of stability and nimble

handling. Mindful of rider comfort over America's wide-open spaces, a deeply sprung seat was included. Indians were equipped with a left-hand throttle, which was said to be a concession to riders who wanted to ride and shoot pistols simultaneously!

In 1928 and 1929, Indian won every American national championship. Unfortunately,

Between the Wars

hour (161kph). Like the Indian Model 101, the famed two-cammers fell victim to the Depression. By 1930, Harley had stopped producing them, making the JH and especially the larger JDH among the most desirable classic Harleys.

It is interesting to compare the big Harleys with the motorcycles available to the British sporting gent. Norton had won the Senior TT in 1924 with an overhead-valve 500cc single. The Norton Model 18 was the "production" version of this machine, and as word of the victory spread, Norton dealers were swamped. In 1926, the Model 18's reputation was bolstered again when

the great Stanley Woods rode it to another win in the Senior—his first of ten.

A year later, Norton built a special overhead-cam version of the 18 called the CS1. This was the grandfather of the famous Norton Internationals, and a customer version of the CS1 was available by early 1928. Published figures for the early overhead-valve models list 18 horsepower and a top speed of 85 miles per hour (137kph). If claims of a top speed of 100 miles per hour (161kph) for the overhead-cam version are to be believed, it must have produced about 25 horsepower.

It may not be entirely fair to compare the Norton with the Harley JDH. After all, the Harley is a road bike with a "race-inspired" engine, while the "cammy" Norton was a full-fledged (and rare!) race replica. Still, the British bike developed 90 percent of the Harley's power with only 40 percent of the displacement. Girder forks may not have offered a significant advantage over the Harley's springers, but the Norton enjoyed a weight advantage of at least 100 pounds (45.5kg). It is hard to imagine hustling a JDH, with its foot clutch and hand-shift controls, around the Isle of Man at the lap speeds of 60 miles per hour (96.5kph) that Stan Woods averaged on his single.

British designers did not limit their originality to the track. In 1930, Edward Turner—who in just

Left: **1929 Harley JD. 74 cubic inches. Unencumbered by its sidecar, this may have been the fastest mass production vehicle of its day. It was the first H-D model to feature a front brake.** *Below:* **The 1938 Senior TT. Stan Woods (Velocette) with Harold Daniell and Freddie Frith (Nortons). Daniell won the race at an average speed of 91 mph (146.4kph), 50 percent faster than the winning time ten years earlier.**

a few years would become the most influential man in motorcycling—created an utterly original motorcycle in the form of his Ariel Square Four.

Turner wanted to build a luxury touring motorcycle that didn't produce the numbing vibration of the big singles and V-twins that were then popular. In-line four-cylinder engines offered smoothness, but were too bulky. Turner responded by mating a pair of vertical twins front to back. The engine featured a twin-crank similar to modern Grand Prix motorcycles, as well as twin overhead cams. Around 1932, the motorcycle business slumped throughout Britain, and Ariel was briefly in receivership. The company fortunately recovered, and this outstanding design was produced

for almost thirty years, in a variety of sizes ranging from 500 to 1000cc.

Back in America, however, the early thirties were no mere slump. In 1933, Harley-Davidson shipped only four thousand motorcycles, about one-fifth of its pre-WWI volume. Excelsior gave up motorcycles for bicycles in 1931. Indian, though it would exist for another twenty years, was being drained by financiers who had no love for motorcycles. If Harley-Davidson had not still been controlled by its founders, it too might have fallen by the wayside.

Roosevelt's New Deal may have inspired a cautious optimism in the mid-thirties, as Harley-Davidson released an innovative new engine with many modern features. It came to be known as

the Knucklehead because the rocker covers were thought to resemble two knuckles. The 1000cc Knucklehead was the first of Harley's signature V-twins to feature overhead valves and a recirculating lubrication system.

The first few years of the E Series (as the Knuckleheads were officially known) were marked by troubles with the new oil system and a less-than-smooth transition to unionized labor at the Milwaukee factory. By 1941, the factory was up to speed for the introduction of the 1200cc version, which served Harley well for more than forty

Opposite, top: **The Turner-designed Ariel Square Four engine was released as a 500cc model in 1930. It grew to 600cc in '32, and reached 1000cc in 1936.** *Opposite, bottom:* **The Square Four was originally sold with girder forks and a rigid frame. Rear plunger suspension was introduced in 1939, and telescopic forks followed in 1946. This model is c.1950.** *Above:* **1934 Harley VL with compact, side-valve 74 ci engine.** *Right:* **1939 "Knucklehead" motor. The first versions of this ohv engine were plagued with stubborn lubrication problems.**

years before lending its basic design to the current Harley-Davidson Evolution motors.

The E Series Harleys were really the last of the motorcycles designed, produced, and marketed under the careful eyes of the founders. William

Davidson died in 1937; his brother Walter, who had been the chief tester in the early days, died five years later, and the year after that, designer Bill Harley passed away. World War II interrupted the production of the Knucklehead, and it was a long time before postwar Harleys reached the finish quality found in the handful of 1941 and 1942 models, now highly prized by collectors.

Only Indian remained to contest the American market, and in the period before World War II, the tourer they pitted against the Knucklehead was the venerable Indian 4. This design had originated as the Henderson around 1911. Bill Henderson sold the rights to the design to Excelsior and then founded the Ace Motorcycle Company, where he continued to develop the basic in-line four inlet-over-exhaust valve engine. Henderson died in 1922, and in 1927 Indian purchased the assets of Ace.

Indian's contribution to the design included one ill-fated effort to revamp the head into an exhaust-over-inlet pattern in 1936. In 1938, they reverted to the original engine layout, and limited themselves to making it look "more like an Indian."

By 1941, the Indian 4 was a motorcycle in a zoot suit: long, low, and ensconced in deeply skirted fenders. It was an old smoothy, but no matter how it was dressed up, it was hopelessly out of date. It didn't matter anyway—Japan's attack on Pearl Harbor was about to pitch America headlong into war.

Across the Atlantic, the Battle of Britain already raged. But on the eve of war, Edward Turner (then designing for Triumph) had shown the world the future of motorcycling. It must have been a long war for motorcyclists as they waited to get their hands on a Triumph Speed Twin.

Turner's design services were acquired for Triumph when Jack Sangster, who had saved Ariel in 1932, bought a controlling interest in Triumph in 1936. Turner must have set to work immediately, as his first new Triumph, a 500cc vertical twin, was released to immediate acclaim in 1937. The Speed Twin design seems shockingly modern next to other prewar motorcycles. It was to

Above: **The Battle of Britain already raged before America entered the war, throwing its motorcycle industry into disarray for the second time in twenty-five years.** *Left:* **Walter Davidson was Harley-Davidson's development rider in the early years. In this 1908 photo, he poses with a machine he used to win an FAM (Federation of American Motorcyclists) endurance competition. Walter died in 1942.**

In the years leading up to World War I, Harley-Davidson fielded a large works racing effort, the participants of which came to be known as the "Wrecking Crew." This nickname reflected the fact that, when they showed up at a race, the weekend was wrecked for all other competitors! This was a period of continued innovation on the part of Harley-Davidson. William Harley admitted that there were more engineers in the racing department than were involved in the development of production machines! The Wrecking Crew raced right through World War I and were increasingly dominant until 1921, when Harley took every event in the U.S. national championship. Then, with the entire U.S. motorcycle industry in recession, the factory withdrew from racing.

Harley-Davidson dealers continued to supply machines to racers, and through the 1920s Indian and Excelsior maintained full factory efforts. All focused on the dirt ovals that constituted the American championship. In 1924 and 1926, the AMA rules restricted Class A racing to 350cc in the interests of improved safety. In 1931, Excelsior shut down and their star rider, Joe Petrali, moved to Harley-Davidson riding a 350cc overhead-valve single Peashooter. Harley backed him with a full works effort, and Petrali won the championship in 1931, 1932, 1933, 1935, and 1936.

In 1934, the AMA introduced Class C racing for production-based motorcycles. This became the premier class in American racing within a couple of years. With the encouragement of Harley and Indian, who were eager to cut the cost of developing increasingly potent 350s, Class A was abolished in 1938. Both Harley and Indian marketed "racing" versions of their 750cc side-valve twins for Class C, Harley the anemic WL and Indian the fine Sport Scout.

The American penchant for dirt tracks was in sharp contrast to racing in Europe, which was conducted mainly on public roads. European manufacturers, competing at places

Above: **Labor Day, 1925, Laurel, Maryland. Joe Petrali, who would become America's biggest motorcycle racing star in the 1930s, is on the right.** *Below:* **Using skills honed on American dirt tracks, Kenny Roberts became the first American to win the World Championship.**

like the Isle of Man, were forced to develop technology that transferred much more directly into their production machines. Improved suspension, smaller, high-revving power plants in nimble chassis, and larger brakes were all developed in the quest for trophies. Unlike America, where the exhausted manufacturers had colluded to minimize the cost of competition, European competition was fierce. In the eighteen years between the wars, no fewer than eight marques won the Senior TT.

The difference between these two approaches is especially evident when one compares the BMW Kompressor used to win the 1939 TT with a Harley WR racer of the same period. With its telescopic forks, plunger rear suspension, and supercharged, dual-overhead-cam engine, the BMW is still up to date. The Harley has a rigid frame, springer forks, and a sidevalve engine, and seems to have emerged from some altogether different, vanished time.

It is interesting to wonder what motorcycles the American industry would have produced had they been racing on roads and the Europeans on dirt. Would Indian's Sport Scout have evolved, by now, into a thoroughbred roadster like a modern Ducati?

To be fair to the Americans, the bikes they raced were appropriate technological solutions for the dirt tracks. After all, brakes were not even allowed in dirt-track racing until 1969 (!) and the broad powerband of the low-revving Class C bikes was ideal for "rear-wheel steering" on the throttle.

In any case, while Europeans may have laughed at dirt-track machines, no one laughed at dirt-track riders. From the earliest days, dirt racers displayed surprising turns of speed during their occasional ventures onto pavement. In the 1970s, when Kenny Roberts became the first American world champion, the Europeans grumbled that he had a distinct advantage: his sliding, dirt-track style ideally suited the tire-spinning 500cc Grand Prix motorcycles.

Above: **1941 Indian Four. Wartime metal shortages drove the price of this model to an astronomical $965.** *Right:* **1937 Speed Twin. The first "modern" motorcycle. During the war, this engine was fitted with aluminum cylinders, and used as an electrical generator in Lancaster bombers. That lightweight motor was then used to win the first postwar TT.**

remain in production for the next forty years with only detail changes.

Turner's was not the first parallel twin, but it was the first to get things right. With pistons moving in unison, it offered no advantage in terms of balance over a single-cylinder design, but the lighter pistons, rods, and valvetrain enabled it to spin to 6000 rpm, good for 26 horsepower. The two cams were mounted high, reducing pushrod mass, and the short crankshaft allowed for an engine case that was actually narrower than many singles of the day.

Had the war not intervened, the other manufacturers would have had competing twins on the market in a few years, but it would be the 1950s before the full impact of Turner's design would be felt.

C
h
a
p
t
e
r

3

Peace
Returns
to
Europe

Europe's motorcycle industry picked itself up and dusted itself off after World War II. As always, war had sharpened the engineers' imaginations, but brilliant new ideas sometimes ran ahead of bombed-out manufacturers' capabilities. British production had been hurt in the blitz; in return, the Allies' daylight raids had reduced the Axis factories to rubble.

In Britain, rationing was still in force, and a tremendous pent-up demand was held in check by a government desperate for exports, which were needed to pay war debts. First in Italy and then Germany (as occupying armies relaxed their control of German industry), motorcycle factories began to produce the sort of affordable, practical motorcycles that Europe needed to get moving again.

British manufacturers immediately lobbied the Federation Internationale Motocycliste (FIM) and succeeded in having supercharging banned. This technology, which had been used to good effect by the Germans and Italians immediately before the war, was a temporary measure, as everyone realized that high-technology, multicylinder engines would eventually outperform the thumping singles made in England. However, there were foundations to pour and new tools on order, and for the time being, developments of prewar machines would have to do. Norton prepared for the 1947

Pages 40–41: **1946 Indian Chief. The plunger-sprung frame appeared on Indians during the war. The deeply valenced fenders were functional, keeping rain and dirt off riders, but some complained that they made the motorcycle too susceptible to crosswinds.** *Left:* **"Boy's Racer" AJS 7R. The overhead cam engine and liberal use of lightweight alloys marked this as a true production racer. In the right hands, it was capable of winning Grands Prix.** *Below:* **Vincent Black Shadow. This is a late-model Series C, produced in 1954. For a full decade after World War II, this machine set the standard for motorcycle performance and build quality.** *Opposite, Right:* **1948 Harley WL. This 45 ci model was the basis for many Harley racers in the postwar years. Its strong bottom end was also grafted into Indian Scout racers. These were known as "big base" Scouts, and displaced 52cc, in flagrant violation of AMA Class C rules.** *Opposite, top:* **During the war years, Norton devoted all of its production to the side valve 16H, seen here with sidecar-mounted machine gun. This option was cut from the Norton catalog when hostilities ended.**

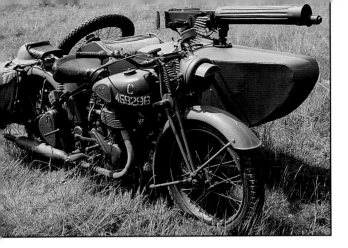

TT by fine-tuning the factory bikes from 1938; in the intervening years the company had been occupied with the production of sixty thousand WD16H military machines.

Stateside, returning GIs are said to have bought Harleys and formed the first "outlaw" motorcycle gangs. Harley-Davidson ended the war on its best financial footing in decades, but maintaining the status quo must have seemed good enough, with Indian—Harley's only real competition—faltering on their own.

If postwar motorcyclists were limited to prewar designs, one design, at least, offered raw performance that street bikes would not exceed for a generation: the Vincent Black Shadow. When *Motor Cycle* tested the Shadow in the summer of 1949, the magazine was unreserved in its praise: "It is a connoisseur's machine, one with speed and acceleration far greater than those of any standard motor cycle; and it is a motor cycle with unique and ingenious features which make it one of the outstanding designs of all time."

The Vincent H.R.D. Company was formed in 1928, when Phil Vincent bought the assets of a motorcycle company owned by racer-designer Howard Davies. Davies' motorcycles were well thought of, and his company was known by his

initials, H.R.D. Years later, the lucky few Vincent owners joked that those initials stood for "Harley Rider's Dream."

The Black Shadow was Vincent's top-of-the-line road machine and the basis for the Black Lightning racer. Modified slightly to run on alcohol, these motorcycles set several world speed records for

unstreamlined machines. Photos of rider Rollie Free on the Bonneville Salt Flats in 1948 show him, at 157 miles per hour (253kph), wearing only a bathing suit to minimize wind resistance!

Vincent's creation is a marvel of both technology and style. The overhead-valve V-twin is fully stressed, with the only "frame" being a box-section tube (which doubles as the oil reservoir) that connects the steering head to the rear suspension pickup. The rear swing arm is bolted to the unit-construction engine/gearbox. The front suspension is Vincent's "girdraulic" unit, while twin rear shocks are mounted horizontally beneath the seat.

Phil Vincent was one of the very first to recognize the potential of rear "swinging fork" suspension, but he had trouble convincing the public of its merits. In Roy Harper's *The Vincent H.R.D. Story*, Phil Vincent is quoted as saying, "You were thought of as a complete maniac if you rode a

Peace Returns to Europe

sprung-frame machine. People told you they were waiting to attend your funeral, which wasn't very encouraging. The prejudice was so great, we had to make the spring frame look as much like a rigid frame as possible, so we tucked it [the spring] away under the saddle."

Vincents made extensive use of stainless steel, and the black tanks, black-enamel engines, and sparse gold accents created a muscular, meant-for-business image that is as evocative now as it was in 1955, when financial considerations brought production to a halt. Right to the end, build quality was superb; it is said that more than half of all Vincents are still in rideable condition. Vincent owners are acutely aware of the magical pull these machines continue to have, and the bikes are thus more likely to remain family heirlooms than come onto the market.

In Italy, Moto Guzzi had been one of the most successful motorcycle manufacturers before the war, and the company was among the first to get back on its feet after it. Since the twenties, the mainstay of the Moto Guzzi line had been a series of elegant 500cc singles, with a characteristic horizontal engine layout. In the postwar years, this motorcycle was built in road versions, like the Astore, and production racing versions, like the Dondolino.

Guzzi's horizontal cylinder centered all of the engine's weight along the ideal line between the hubs, which helped the bikes to handle well. An idiosyncratic rear suspension layout relied on a tension spring beneath the engine. Combined with the "oversquare" bore and stroke of 88 x 82mm, which was ahead of its time, this was a basic design that Moto Guzzi was able to produce for more than fifty years.

With a more conventional chassis and a more potent engine, the British Velocette KTT was establishing itself as a force to be reckoned with on racing circuits during the late forties. Before the war, Velocette had been among the most innovative British manufacturers. It produced an over-

Opposite, far left: **In 1950, Rollie Free rode this unstreamlined Vincent to a then-record 156.71 mph (251kph). In order to minimize air resistance, Free stripped to bathing briefs for his record attempts!** *Opposite, top:* **1949 Vincent HRD. Polished engine cases identify this as the "Rapide" model.** *Opposite, bottom:* **Prewar Velocette KTT, 350cc. Early Velocette overhead cam racers inspired Norton and others to abandon pushrod designs. The fishtail muffler on this bike is known as a "Brooklands" exhaust. The British circuit had more stringent noise limits than other tracks.** *Above:* **A c.1940 Indian Scout. With the exception of its modern alloy wheels, this would have been a typical dirt track racer in the postwar period.**

head-cam racer in 1925 that inspired the Norton CS1, then broke new ground in 1936 with a double-overhead-cam engine, which again raised the stakes. Its most lasting contribution to motorcycling may have been the "positive-stop" foot gearchange, which gave Velocette racers a decided advantage and which was quickly copied.

Velocette took the 1949 and 1950 350cc world championships on a twin-cam "factory special" version of the KTT, which had changed little from before the war. It was still equipped with somewhat dated friction-damped girder forks, and the rear suspension consisted of a swing arm and pressurized air/oil shocks.

The KTT production racer is the prized Velo, as it was one of the first motors to approach the theoretical power limits of the single-cylinder design. The overhead-valve road machines are also highly sought after and admired for their modern handling and ride comfort.

Velocette's principal competition among production racers in the popular 350cc class was the AJS 7R. This was also known as the "Boy's Racer,"

and entered production in 1949. Before the war AJS had fielded a fast, technically impressive and water-cooled V4 with overhead cams, but it had relied on supercharging, which was now against the rules. Showing impressive development abilities, AJS quickly fielded the nonsupercharged Porcupine twin for their works riders and used it to win the 500cc world championship in 1949. The Porcupine, however, didn't live up to its early promise. The factory stopped building custom works machines in 1954 to concentrate on the sales of their production racers, which were then the choice of many Grand Prix privateers.

With its double-cradle frame, telescopic forks, and rear swing arm, the 7R established a general layout for both racing and road motorcycles.

At the conclusion of World War II, Germany was left bombed out, divided, and under the control of several occupying armies. The Russians moved quickly to impose Communism on the area under their control. German industry was further hampered by the loss of patents, which were taken as "war reparations."

Among these patents were the formulation for aspirin, the world's most popular headache remedy, and the design of the world's most popular motorcycle, the DKW RT125. Both BSA and Harley-Davidson were aware that they lacked such a "utility" motorcycle for their domestic markets and seized the chance to have DKW-pattern bikes in production by 1948.

DKW had been building motorcycles in Zschopau, Germany, since 1919. By the thirties, DKW was proving itself particularly adept at the creation of small, powerful two-strokes. They were successful in the marketplace and on the race track, fielding works bikes with innovative forced induction systems.

After the war, Harley-Davidson built a copy of the popular little 125, which they called the Hummer. Later versions, which H-D equipped with telescopic forks, were called Tele-Glides. Intended for use as around-town runabouts, Hummers could be purchased from Harley-Davidson for as little as $5.50 per week. The BSA Bantam was another DKW copy, which was more of a commercial success than its American cousin. More than half a million Bantams were produced between 1948 and 1971, during which time they became the standard

Above: **1972 MZ Trophy. Degner's defection and the theft of MZ's trade secrets did not harm MZ's production of utilitarian machines like this one.** *Below:* **1938 BSA Silver Star 350. The postwar BSA Bantam, a DKW copy, was a huge success.**

mode of transportation for the British blue-collar worker.

By 1949, many of DKW's workers had fled to West Germany, and the DKW factory, then part of Auto Union (now known as Audi), reopened in Ingolstadt. The old factory and some of the old employees continued operations under the East German planned economy as IFA and, later, MZ.

MZ (Motorradwerke Zschopau) was hampered by having to operate within East Germany's planned economy, and certainly didn't have access to the budgets, materials, and motivated labor force that DKW had. However, the MZ factory was soon producing two-stroke racers that were coveted by Grand Prix riders in the fifties and sixties.

The rise of the MZ racing program can be traced to one man, Walter Kaaden, who took over the racing department in 1953. Kaaden is a titan of two-stroke engine development, and every modern Grand Prix engine owes half its horsepower to his creative genius.

He replaced the old forced induction systems of DKW with disc valves and then invented the modern "expansion chamber" exhaust, which uses resonance to improve combustion chamber filling and

scavenging. In 1954, MZ race engines could produce about 100 horsepower per liter of displacement. By 1961, Kaaden's engines were producing 200 hp/liter, a figure that even the mammoth Japanese factories would not improve for twenty years.

In 1958 and 1959, MZ finished second and third in the 250cc world championship. MZ's success was a major propaganda coup for East Germany. They reveled in the fact that capitalist riders as well known as Luigi Taveri, Derek Minter, and Mike Hailwood sought out MZs to race, even though other manufacturers offered cash inducements. Ernst Degner, a homegrown rider, was poised on the brink of major stardom. Then in 1961, with MZ leading the 125cc championship, Degner defected. He made his escape at the Swedish Grand Prix. Within hours, he was on his way to Japan, where he was signed to ride for Suzuki.

The next year, Suzuki's power and reliability improved dramatically, and Degner won the 50cc title. It was the first world championship won on a two-stroke since the war. In 1963, Hugh Anderson followed this up with Suzuki's second win, in the 125cc class. Everyone who saw the new Suzuki engines was struck by their similarity to Walter Kaaden's designs. Rumors circulated that Degner had escaped with plans or even a whole MZ engine. The truth may never be known; some years later, Degner committed suicide.

It is interesting to think what might have developed had other German designs been adopted by the Allies after the war. The Russian Cossack factory attempted a BMW flat twin, as did the French, but neither has stood the test of time. If only Indian, instead of attempting to develop its own "British-style" vertical twin, had taken on the BMW flat twin instead! They could have adopted a tried and tested design ideally suited to open-road cruising without incurring the new engine development costs that bankrupted the company after the war.

Extensive use of magnesium alloy components brought the weight down to less than 300 pounds (136kg). With more than 30 horsepower on tap, the overhead-cam engine would push the bike to speeds of 110 miles per hour (177kph).

AJS had produced motorcycles since 1909 but was sold to Matchless in 1931. The new company came to be known as Associated Motor Cycles, and it was to figure prominently in the rationalization of the British motorcycle industry after the war. Sunbeam was temporarily under the AMC umbrella, as were James and Francis-Barnett. AMC's most famous acquisition was Norton, in 1953. For a time, AMC management encouraged each company to pursue its own ends (although AJS and Matchless motorcycles shared many components).

In the late fifties, AMC produced both the AJS 7R and its principal competitor, the 350cc Manx Norton. The 7R was even enlarged to create the

1958 Matchless G12. This 650cc touring twin was overshadowed by Triumphs and BSAs. Even this late, the lack of chrome illustrates British post-war materials shortages. Although the G12 used a three-bearing crankshaft (most of the other British twins did not use a middle bearing), its brittle crank was prone to spectacular failures.

Matchless G50, which was made expressly to challenge Norton's supremacy in the 500cc class. As the British industry came under increasing pressure, however, the last AJS four-strokes were built in the mid-sixties.

Peace Returns to Europe

After World War II, a successful working man might well have ridden a motorcycle to work, then on the weekend hooked up a one-, two-, or even four-passenger sidecar, loaded up the wife, child, and mother-in-law, and headed into the countryside for a picnic. Sidecars greatly increased the practical value of motorcycles, and they have certainly not been given their due by most collectors. The sidecar had always been an important way to increase the capacity of the motorcycle, but when affordable cars became the choice for family travel in the twenties, the sidecar's popularity in the United States fell off, though it remained a common sight on European roads well into the fifties.

The sturdy, low-geared motorcycles most suited to duty as sidecar "tugs" are also underappreciated. The Panther motorcycles, designed by Phelon and Moore, were particularly fine tugs, equipped with massive 600 to 650cc single-cylinder engines. Phelon and Moore were not quick to adopt change for its own sake, and their basic slant single design changed little from 1925 until 1965. Postwar models are big, handsome machines with twin exhaust ports that make them look like two-cylinder jobs, though they aren't. Sidecar workplaces added strain on the chassis of the tug, but P&M were confident in their castings, as the massive sloping cylinder serves as the front downtube.

Of course, it wasn't long after the first two sidecar-equipped motorcyclists met on the street that sidecar racing took place. A number of early sidecar designs were developed to "lean" with the motorcycle as it cornered at ever-higher speeds. The two basic types were the American FLXI ("flexi") sidecar, which was attached to the motorcycle with a type of hinge, allowing the sidecar to ride level while the bike leaned, and the British Dixon, in which the sidecar passenger tilted the sidecar by pulling on levers.

By the 1930s, the racing sidecar had taken its modern form: essentially a flat platform with hand- and footholds on which the sidecar passenger—sometimes called a "monkey"—scrambled to shift weight to the inside of turns. In truth, the passenger is no mere monkey, but plays a skilled role in balancing the machine during cornering and braking. Notwithstanding this, sidecar manufacturers were frightened by the image of this wild-and-

woolly riding style and actively tried to discourage sidecar racing, as they felt it would frighten away potential customers.

Goulding (United States) and Viceroy (England) were examples of fine, comfortable sidecars, but the Steib sidecars produced in Germany until 1957 are perhaps the most elegant of all.

At this point, we should spare a thought for Indian, which had been terminal for some time by the late 1940s. After the war, Indian correctly

anticipated the popularity of the lighter, sportier British singles and twins, and embarked on several such designs. These motorcycles proved unexpectedly difficult to build, and early versions had a variety of quality-control problems.

To their credit, Indian didn't admit defeat. In 1948 and 1949, Floyd Emde won at Daytona on a Sport Scout, but only a handful of these bikes were manufactured. After the war, the Chief, which had been an Indian mainstay since the

Opposite, top left: **1961 Francis-Barnett Falcon. This 200cc two-stroke was typical of the millions of small motorcycles that provided basic transportation for the British working class. It was not until the early 1960s that automobile registrations exceeded motorcycle registrations in Britain.** *Opposite, right:* **Detail, 1948 Indian Chief.** *Opposite, bottom:* **Sidecar racers at the old Avus race course, near Berlin, c.1935. This racing sidecar is a flat platform, with prominent handholds for its daring passenger.** *Below:* **1946 Harley-Davidson "Knucklehead."**

Above: **The fact that the Indian trademark continued to appear on cheap minibikes into the 1970s gave the great brand's fans the cruel hope that "real" Indians would someday ride again.** *Right:* **Royal Enfield "Bullet" 350. Enfield twins were among the first roadsters to adopt rear swingarm suspension. After the collapse of the British motorcycle industry, Enfield's tooling was sold to an Indian Company, which continues to produce and sell this model.**

twenties, was updated for the last time. The leaf-spring front suspension was finally replaced by a girder unit, and a rear plunger was added. The hand shift and left-hand throttle were retained.

With their deeply skirted fenders, huge tanks, and softly sprung seats, the last Chiefs are the quintessential American motorcycles. The 74-cubic-inch Chief and the 80-cubic-inch Blackhawk Chief were produced into the early fifties.

Indian was sold to Brockhouse, an English holding company that momentarily owned AMC. For a time, Brockhouse brought in Royal Enfields, which were badged as Indians. In the sixties, things got even worse, as the famous trademark was applied to lawnmower-engined minibikes. For years, stories that the tooling for the Chief had been stored gave many Indian fans the cruel hope that the brand might be resurrected.

Peace Returns to Europe

C
h
a
p
t
e
r

4

The
Modern
Chassis
Takes
Shape

In the evolution of the motorcycle, it has been rare for any one machine to be innovative in both chassis and engine design. Normally, advancement in one area spurs designers to improvements in the other. A more powerful engine, for example, overstrains the chassis. An improved chassis is built, and old speeds (once fast enough, thank you very much) seem slower. Where the previous engine had been adequate, riders now crave even more power; when they get it, they need stronger brakes, and on and on.

In the early 1950s, the development of the motorcycle had split at the English Channel. On the Continent, manufacturers were picking up where they had left off before the war. Their focus was on the develpment of more complex and more powerful multicylinder engines. By 1955, several builders would prove the viability of the across-the-frame four-cylinder engine, which still dominates current thinking.

In England, in 1950, motorcycling saw the future of chassis design; the combination of a stiff, double-loop frame, telescopic forks, and a rear swing arm with hydraulic damping set the standard for the next twenty-five years. On the race tracks, these were days of comparatively underpowered British "thumpers" gaining in the bends, while howling Italian multis pulled away down the straights. They were great days for motorcycle builders. Sales were brisk. Some manufacturers failed to modernize and faded from the scene, but for the most part, Europe's demand for cheap transportation seemed insatiable.

Cars were still out of reach for millions of working families. The most profitable sectors of the motorcycle industry were affordable, practical scooters and mopeds. Flush with cash from sales of utility motorcycles, the European manufacturers entered Grands Prix with ever more exotic racing machines, which often bore no resemblance to the bikes coming off their assembly lines.

Record sales lay ahead, but a close observer of the British industry would see little technological advance from this point on. The mighty British motorcycle industry was ignoring its own automobile industry, a flood of cheap imports from Europe, and the sleeping giant in Japan.

The Norton team had much to fear entering 1950. Joe Craig, their racing manager, had designed the AJS Porcupine twin that won the championship the previous year, so he knew its potential. Gilera, too, unveiled ever more powerful multis. Norton's own 500cc single was already long in the tooth, with only marginal improvements to come. Competing on horsepower was out of the question.

To make matters worse, Norton's "garden gate" frame was heavy, prone to breakage, and offered no great advantage in handling. Fortunately, the McCandless brothers, a pair of Irish racing

Pages 52–53: **1962 Triumph T120 R. British versions had flat handlebars (as shown), while machines destined for export to America had higher handlebars. The tachometer drive seen on the right-side crankcase was standard equipment on U.S. versions, but was often fitted by British riders as an aftermarket accessory.** *Opposite top:* **1954 Harley KH. Compact and brawny-looking, it was hampered by an outdated side-valve engine. This model would later form the basis for the visually similar Sportster.** *Opposite, bottom:* **Postwar Norton International, with the plunger-sprung "garden gate" frame. This was the starting point for British postwar racing motorcycles, c.1948.** *Above:* **1957 350cc Norton Manx. Compared to the "garden gate" frame, the "featherbed" frame was lighter, stiffer, and offered far greater rider comfort. Thirty-five horsepower pushed this 310-pound (115kg) machine to a top speed of 115 mph (185kph).** *Below:* **Geoff Duke, at speed on his Championship-winning four-cylinder Gilera 500, 1954.**

mechanics, delivered Norton a ready-made solution to the problem. The McCandless chassis wasn't the very first of its kind; rather, it was the first of its kind to get things just right. Harold Daniell, a Norton works rider, was brought in to test the new machine, and when he pulled in he said it was as comfortable "as a featherbed." Thus, the famous Norton featherbed frame was christened.

The McCandless brothers had welded up a sturdy, double-loop frame. Norton "Roadholder" forks were mounted up front, and at the rear a swing arm replaced the old plunger unit. The rear shocks attached to a subframe. Roadholding and

rider comfort were so dramatically improved that Norton's works engines were all immediately installed in featherbed frames. Geoff Duke won the TT with the design right off the bat. Early versions were manufactured by the McCandless brothers at their workshop in Ireland. By 1952, Norton was offering the featherbed on production racers and then on road bikes. Reynolds, the tubing specialists, undertook mass production.

The featherbed frame provided Norton's old International production racer with a new lease on life. The engines in the works bikes were evolutions of the twin-overhead-cam CS2 motor, but the proddy bikes featured a single overhead camshaft. Gradually, these engines got larger bores and shorter strokes, enabling them to rev higher. To better market their superb performances (especially on the Isle of Man), Norton began calling these classic 350 and 500cc singles Manx Nortons.

The Manx was always a real production racer, and was produced in small quantities—about 150 a year from 1952 until the early 1960s. It is unlikely that any model made before or since had more Grand Prix starts. The deafening flat exhaust note of a Manx going into a corner makes

The Modern Chassis Takes Shape

A 1954 film that starred Marlon Brando, with Lee Marvin in a supporting role, The Wild One was inspired by the Hollister, California, motorcycle riot of 1947. This film served as the prototype for an entire genre of "biker" movies. It opens with scenes of a sullen, brooding Johnny (Brando) riding a Triumph Thunderbird into a small town, accompanied by a gang of bikers who resemble beatniks decked out in black leather.

Trouble brews when these charming rogues are confronted by Lee Marvin, riding a Harley Hydra-Glide and leading a (rather dirtier and more drunken) rival gang. A fight breaks out when Chino (Marvin) steals Johnny's racing trophy. While the fight has little to do with motorcycles, the conflict foreshadows the heyday of British motorcycles in America after the war and the difficult times ahead for Harley-Davidson, the last surviving U.S. manufacturer.

In reality, the rise of the "outlaw" bike gangs may have been a case of life imitating art, or at least imitating the wildly paranoid media coverage of a handful of well-attended motorcycle races. Whatever the real reason for their existence, the first bike gangs are usually traced to the West Coast in the years immediately after World War II. Hundreds of thousands of GIs were discharged at California ports. With time on their hands and money in their pockets, buying motorcycles no doubt seemed a way to put some excitement back in their lives. The infamous Hell's Angels are said to have taken their name from that of a bomber squadron in which they flew together.

At the conclusion of World War I, Allied soldiers brought back stories of how powerful and reliable the American Harleys and Indians had been compared to the European military-issue bikes. It was dif-

Above: **Marlon Brando as the misunderstood "Johnny" in** *The Wild One.* **The movie outraged the motorcycle industry in 1954; they complained that all motorcyclists were slandered by the portrayal of a tiny minority of "outlaw bikers." Triumph sales skyrocketed, however.** *Below:* **1952 Harley-Davidson Hydra Glide.** *Opposite, top:* **1952 Triumph Thunderbird 650** *Opposite, middle:* **The Hell's Angels, 1966** *Opposite, bottom:* **1947 Triumph 3T, 350cc. The smaller Triumphs were handsome machines in their own right, but were rarely seen in the United States.**

ferent the second time around. The European (and particularly British) engineering philosophy of a lighter bike, with a smaller, free-revving engine, had made converts of many Americans. Many GIs now found the big V-twins to be lumbering and inelegant.

Triumph was the first of the British manufacturers to identify this opportunity, and the United States became its biggest market in the postwar years. Immediately before the war, Triumph's inspired, Turner-designed 500cc Speed Twin had shown the world the future of motorcycling. This basic design was adapted to the wide-open spaces of America by upping displacement to 650cc. The American-sounding Thunderbird was introduced in 1950. A high-performance version of this tourer, the T110, was introduced in 1954, and in 1959 the twin-carb Bonneville version was released. Its name commemorated Triumph's record-breaking speed achievements on the Bonneville Salt Flats in Utah. These bikes, with their names drawn from the American West, killed off Indian and staggered H-D. For their part, Triumph 650s survived virtually unchanged for more than twenty years. The differences in Johnny's and Chino's choices of motorcycle highlight the difficult game of catch-up, which H-D found itself in during the postwar period (to say nothing of the bikes ridden by some of the other actors, which include such unlikely "outlaw" mounts as a Matchless!).

Triumphs had all been equipped with telescopic front forks by 1946. At this time, Harley, struggling to update the handling of its bikes, added hydraulic damping to its trademark springer front forks. The Hydra-Glide front end was not available until 1949. At the back wheel, Triumph itself was a little too attached to its ingenious-but-dated sprung hub and did not adopt the rear swing arm until 1955. This, however, was more than H-D offered as they persisted with rigid chassis until the introduction of the aptly named Duo-Glide in 1958.

With such daunting competition, it was not long before H-D were pressing for protective tariffs on motorcycle imports (tariffs which, to be fair, H-D were faced with when exporting their motorcycles in the other direction). Its initial attempt to have motorcycle import duties raised from 10 to 40 percent was unsuccessful, and after rousing both Triumph and the U.S. Congress, Harley found itself the victim of several rulings on unfair competition, which ultimately forced it to abandon dealer-exclusivity contracts.

Far from Turner's influence and aware of the American dictum "Win on Sunday, sell on Monday," Triumph U.S.A. pursued trophies and records more aggressively than the head office. Notwithstanding Turner's disdain for racing, the Speed Twin, with a lightweight engine

dominated the record books, holding dozens of records in the restricted classes.

The year of <u>The Wild One</u> was also the first year in which the AMA Grand National Championship was decided by points accumulated over races on both ovals and road courses. Harley dominated the series, winning the first nine titles, but its grip on Daytona, the single most important event, was already weakening. Nortons won from 1949 to 1952. It was Harley-Davidson in 1953 and BSA in 1954, and then Harley had a seven-year victory string. In 1961, racing at Daytona moved from the beach to the speedway, which paved the way for Don Burnett to win on a Triumph the following year. Buddy Elmore and Gary Nixon won again on Triumph Tigers in 1966 and 1967.

In 1968, the other manufacturers forced the AMA to allow all engine designs the full 750cc displacement. This unleashed the new Triumph Trident triple, which produced 80 horsepower and had a considerable advantage over the 65-horsepower H-D KR. Down on power, Rayborn conserved his bike for popular wins at the 1968 and 1969 Daytona races, but they were to be Harley's swan song on pavement. By 1971, the Daytona podium was fully occupied by riders of British triples, as Triumph-derived BSA Rocket 3s took first and third, with a Triumph Trident second.

repeatedly set by Triumph, as the record was pushed up from 214 miles per hour (344kph) to more than 245 miles per hour (394kph). Finally, in 1970, Triumph relinquished the outright record to a Harley-powered projectile piloted by legendary racer Cal Rayborn, but Triumph still

(developed during the war for use as a generator on Lancaster bombers) was campaigned successfully, including winning the Senior TT in 1946, when racing resumed after the war.

This version of the Tiger was exported to the United States, where it was also raced with some success. Harley-Davidson, however, had more pull with the American Motorcycle Association than it had with Congress, and had ensured that the rules of Class C racing (the most popular class) favored the machines from Milwaukee by allowing side-valve engines to displace 750cc, while overhead-valve engines, such as those used by Triumph, were limited to 500cc.

These disadvantages did not apply to speed record attempts. Between 1955 and 1970, Triumph's marketing department benefited from a series of well-publicized record attempts on the Bonneville Salt Flats. During that period, the motorcycle land speed record was

The Modern Chassis Takes Shape

modern race bikes sound anemic, and in that note enthusiasts hear the echoes of great champions such as Geoff Duke, Mike Hailwood, and John Surtees. The Manx is the platonic essence of racing motorcycles, one of the most prized classics.

Norton was eager to build road-going machines on the featherbed frame, and a combination of this chassis with a vertical-twin engine was the marketing department's dream. Bert Hopwood set out to create Norton's answer to Triumph's Speed Twin, and his solution, in 1952, was the 500cc Norton Dominator. This engine would remain in production for twenty-five years. Hopwood, knowing it had weaknesses even at 30 horsepower, would have been surprised to know it would finally displace more than 800cc and produce 60 hp!

The Dominator was not widely available in the home market until the model was nearly ten years old. The Labour Government needed export revenue to pay war debts (mainly to the United States). To ensure these exports, the government directed critical raw materials, which were still in scarce supply, to companies that were then forced to use those materials in products for the export market only. Consumer credit was also tightly controlled, and artificially high interest rates meant that new motorcycles were out of reach for most people. At the annual Earl's Court Motorcycle Show, British manufacturers displayed their flagship machines, but to the frustration of British riders the machines were all labeled "For Export Only." Today, motorcycles that were made in England but couldn't be sold there, like early Dominators, are sought after by British collectors.

If an average Joe could only dream of pulling up to the coal pit for his morning shift on a "Domi,"

Opposite: **1962 Norton Dominator 88SS, 650cc. Norton produced sports-touring twins with the featherbed frame from 1952. The original 500cc motor was bored out until it reached the limits of vibration and reliability. This machine appears to have been fitted with a twin leading shoe front brake, of the type found on the Commando, which superseded the "Domi" in the late 1960s.** *Above:* **1949 BSA Bantam D1. Like the Harley-Davidson Hummer, the Bantam was based on patents and designs which the Germans lost after World War II. The Hummer was perceived as a toy in America, but BSA sold over half a million Bantams in Britain.**

what he really rode was likely a BSA Bantam. BSA was quick to take advantage of access to the rugged little DKW RT125 and had their version in production by 1948. BSA sold thousands of Bantams every month for decades. Since England had virtually no highways until the 1960s, it is likely that the Domi would have won out on pose value, but the little Bantam would beat it on practicality anyway.

From 1948 until 1971, BSA made few changes to the Bantam engine unit. Bore size was gradually increased, and displacement went from 125 to 175cc. The Bantam D1 was originally supplied with a rigid frame. A plunger rear suspension was offered later as an option. Its 4-horsepower engine gave it a top speed of about 50 miles per hour (80.5kph). Even this, of course, was enough to bring out the competitive instincts of some Bantam riders. BSA responded with "sports" and "trials" versions, which had swing arm suspensions and engines making a breathtaking 12 hp.

Few Bantam racers could realistically aspire to ride in Grands Prix. However, the 1950s saw several new racing circuits open in Britain, usually on decommissioned military airfields. The grassroots racing that took place on these tracks came to be known as "clubman" racing, and it was very popular. BSA seized the clubman market with a production racer with lights called the BSA Gold

Star. On any summer weekend, hundreds of young Brits would ride their Goldies to the track, remove the lights, race, and then ride home. For a time, there was even a Clubman class at the TT, where as many as 90 percent of the competitors showed up with Gold Stars.

The Gold Star got its name when a BSA Empire Star lapped the Brooklands track at more than 100 miles per hour (161kph) in 1937, earning a gold pin from the Brooklands Motor Cycle Racing Club. Even though BSA was more interested in trials (off-road) competition, they decided to capitalize on the new model's speedy achievement and named it the Gold Star. The war intervened, but when it was over, several Gold Star variants were produced with iron cylinders. In 1948, the first classic Goldie was produced, with an alloy engine and a plunger frame.

In 1952, works Gold Stars produced for the grueling International Six Days Trial experimented with a swing arm rear suspension, which was incorporated into production bikes in 1953.

While most clubmen competed in a single discipline, the Gold Star itself was much more versatile. It could literally, with the exchange of a few parts, compete in trials, motocross, and road races. In 1963, *Motor Cycle* magazine described it as "a straightforward pushrod single, much cheaper to buy than an overhead-camshaft production racer, [but] it nevertheless has a proud race record." Just as important to the amateur, "Maintaining and servicing presents no difficulty to the serious competition rider." The pushrods were operated off two cams, and though the rods were long, Goldies in fairly conservative tune were capable of putting out 40 horsepower and spinning to 7500 rpm. The last Gold Stars were produced in 1962, but they offered amateur racers winning performance and value right to the end.

On the Continent, many club racers favored smaller-displacement bikes, which were cheaper to buy and maintain, but a notable exception was the handsome 500cc single made in Italy by Gilera. Their flagship production bike was the Saturno, which was also sold as a production racer called the Saturno San Remo. Gilera produced about a thousand Saturnos a year after the war, with output slowing to a trickle in the late fifties.

Like the Gold Star, the Saturno has a "user-friendly" pushrod engine, but an automatic spark advance eliminates the risk that the kick starter will launch the rider over the handlebars.

The frame and suspension are a curious combination of old and new. Gilera equipped most Saturnos with an old-style friction damped girder fork, for example, but designed a unit-construction crankcase and gearbox that is a member of the single-downtube cradle frame. A unique rear swing arm relies on friction dampers and a pair of horizontal springs. The rear suspension, especially, looks like something Leonardo da Vinci could

Below: **The BSA Gold Star was manufactured from 1956-62. It was the most versatile Clubman's racer ever made, proving competitive in road racing, motocross, and even trials. While it was not competitive in Grands Prix, a DBD34 similar to this one was used by Dick Mann in road racing events when he won the AMA Championship in 1963.** *Opposite:* **Army issue Harley-Davidson WLA.**

The Modern Chassis Takes Shape

On the image:
SHIP.WGT.-535LBS
O-LGTH-88INS
O-HT-59INS
O-WIDTH-37INS

MILITARY POLICE

USA 7147

have barely figured out. Notwithstanding this unique chassis, Saturnos were lighter than many British singles, had a low center of gravity, and are reported to be "nearly the equivalent of a Manx" in both comfort and handling.

Few Saturnos were raced outside Italy; when Gilera went to Grands Prix, they brought their spectacular four-cylinder machines. These were based on prewar, supercharged Rondine engines, which were licensed by Gilera before the war and which the company had used to win the 1939 world championship. After the war, when supercharging was banned, Gilera went back to the drawing board and developed a design for air-cooled across-the-frame Fours that were the ancestors of most modern superbike engines.

On the track, the Gilera Grand Prix bikes were a handful, to say the least. One of them (just before World War II broke out) was the fastest two-wheeled vehicle on earth, but the frames, suspension, and brakes were not up to the engine's output. At one point, the factory actually built an overhead-cam Saturno for works riders to use on twisty circuits where the multis were a bit much

The Modern Chassis Takes Shape

The Modern Chassis Takes Shape

Opposite: **1948 Lambretta "B", 123cc. Early Lambrettas did not enclose the engine and rear wheel.** *Above:* **The first Grand Prix of 1957. Libero Liberati pilots his dustbin-faired Gilera 350 to victory in Hockenheim, Germany. At the end of the season, Liberati had become the 500cc World Champion.** *Below:* **The 200cc Triumph Tiger Cub was manufactured from 1954. This is a late model, c.1966. Triumph advertised it as "Nippy, easy to handle, and economical to run." Notwith-standing such claims, the Japanese and Italians were more successful at making entry-level motorbikes that appealed to inexperienced riders.**

for even the brilliant Gilera works riders, including the wonderfully named Libero Liberati.

Geoff Duke, in addition to Liberati and Umberto Masetti, won 500cc championships on Gilera multis before the company withdrew from Grand Prix competition in 1957. Duke arrived from Norton, where racers were just "employees." (Stan Woods, who won ten TTs for Norton, was put to work as a salesman for them over the winter!) In Italy, Gilera and MV Augusta works riders were pampered stars. Duke was not just a racer, but a brilliant development rider who, obviously, had great familiarity with the Norton featherbed frame. It is said that under his influence, Gilera's works machines became a little less intimidating to ride.

Guzzi, Gilera, and other Italian makers were busy making "real" motorcycles, but it is possible the most influential development in Italian transportation was the scooter. Scooters had been marketed in the past, but had not caught on, precisely because they were part motorcycle and part car yet not enough of either. It took Italian design flair to redefine the scooter and put it in its own category. Not surprisingly, the designer had no previous experience with motorcycles at all.

Corradino D'Ascanio was a designer with Piaggio, a company that built aircraft until its factory was bombed. D'Ascanio solved the problem of providing Italy with cheap, practical transport by drawing up the famous Vespa scooter from a clean sheet of paper. He began with a comfortable seating position, which didn't require straddling the machine. Footboards and a front "fairing" protected the rider's clothing—essential to style-conscious Italians—and the reliable, simple, two-stroke engine was fully enclosed.

Several of the Vespa's most interesting technical features were drawn from Piaggio's aircraft expertise. The skin is a fully stressed, spot-welded steel stamping. Its complex curves are not only visually pleasing but ensure its rigidity. The small wheels and unique single-sided front suspension unit were based on aircraft landing gear.

Later on, models with rear suspension actually had the entire engine mounted on the swing arm. This lack of concern for unsprung weight and the tricky handling of the tiny wheels made trying to ride a Vespa at "real motorcycle" speeds quite scary. However, its low power and Italy's potholed, war-torn streets served as natural governors. The Vespa was the perfect vehicle for its time, and Piaggio sold them by the millions. In the early 1950s, as many as 80 percent of the vehicles on Italy's roads were scooters!

In short order, other manufacturers took notice. The Lambretta, built by Innocenti, was Vespa's main domestic competitor. The two machines were super-

Above: **Piaggio's amazing little Vespa took post-war Europe by storm.** *Right:* **1958 Cushman Eagle. Cushman built scooters from 1939 onward. Their line ranged from models that were little more than children's toys to utilitarian delivery vehicles. Cushmans never achieved the mass-market popularity of Piaggio or Lambretta.**

ficially similar, but the Lambretta was built on a tube frame and owed more to conventional motorcycle design. Manufacturers in other countries noticed, too, usually after a few hundred thousand of the Italian jobs were sold under their noses. In England, Triumph built the Tigress, which was a real motorcycle, repackaged as a scooter, and a bit of a commercial flop. In America, Cushman had been building scooters since the thirties and sold them through ads in Popular Mechanics. Unfortunately, Cushman built an abomination that looked like a golf cart balanced on two wheels. Only the Germans seemed to get it right. The NSU Prima was based on a licenced Lambretta 150 design, to which the Germans added tasteful chrome accents.

The Modern Chassis Takes Shape

5

The
Continent
Takes
the Lead

To pick one man and call him "the greatest rider of all time" or to choose one motorcycle and say that it is simply "the best ever" is a matter of personal opinion. Not all great riders were contemporary and those who were didn't race on comparable machines. But the records are clear on one thing: between 1949 and 1976, MV Agusta won 275 Grand Prix races. Riders on the fire-engine red machines won thirty-eight individual titles, and MV won thirty-seven manufacturers' championships. There will never, ever be another racing team like MV Agusta.

MV (Meccanica Verghere) made airplanes before the war and later went on to become Europe's largest helicopter builder. Like Piaggio, MV decided to produce affordable transportation during the Italian reconstruction. They began motorcycle production in 1946 with a simple machine that sported a 100cc two-stroke motor.

Agusta was the surname of the factory owner, Count Domenico Agusta. He became enamored with motorcycle racing in the late forties, and then became the patron of the most successful racing team of all time. The Count was the Medici of motorcycling. His team, which at one time fielded sixteen works riders, starred a "Who's Who" of the Classic period, including world champions John Surtees, Phil Read, Giacomo Agostini, and Mike Hailwood. They rode for the pay, the prestige, and the satisfaction of racing for a man who demonstrably loved motorcycles as much as they did. What motorcycles he made! Years later, Surtees wrote in the British magazine *Fast Classics*, "You could actually drive from only 4,000 revs. Things really started to happen at 8,000 and from 10,000 to 14,000 it was superbly progressive,

and all in all with its excellent choice of gear ratios, allowed you to get the right gear and the right revs on virtually any type of corner, particularly vital in a race where everything isn't going to happen exactly as you want or planned. For example, you might well have to take different lines through corners and a totally different approach purely because of other competitors and so this superb relationship between power and chassis is so important."

MV racing machines were designed by Pietro Remor, of Rondine and Gilera fame. Later, Ruggero Mazza created the high-revving, short-stroke engines that were the last four-stroke motors to win in Grand Prix competition. MV's bikes were often Fours, although there were famous triples and some effective single-cylinder 125s.

Looking back on Agusta's passionate racing effort, it all seems very Italian. Brilliant design and fanatical attention to detail created motorcycles that were works of art. But they were also wholly impractical, with the race shop engaging in major casting projects for a single engine, bearing no similarity whatsoever to the motors in MV road bikes.

MV's helicopter business got off the ground quickly, and as a result, the production side of the motorcycle factory didn't get much attention. The best that can be said for its early two-strokes is that they were simple and stylish. For much of the factory's life, the larger street bikes were shaft-driven cruisers. MV's mundane production motorcycles received little marketing impetus from their Grand Prix successes; it was the profits from the helicopter business that fueled the racing program. The only motorcycles MV sold that really reflected

Pages 66–67: **Douglas Dragonfly c.1956. This "love it or hate it" styled 350cc roadster was smooth and handled well. The bike in this photo is fitted with Rodark panniers and a sidecar, which must have strained its 17-horsepower engine.** *Opposite, top:* **Vespa's Italian design epitomized the idea that form follows function, but for British Mods the function of the Vespa was self-expression.** *Opposite, bottom:* **MV's road machines bore only a superficial resemblance to their superb racers. In the early 1970s, many felt that models like this 750S were just an attempt to cash in on the famous Agusta name.** *Above:* **History repeats itself: Giacomo Agostini rides Team Obsolete's MV Agusta 500cc triple at meet in Daytona, 1996. This MV was the last four-stroke to win a Grand Prix.** *Right:* **On an earlier trip to the United States, Ago won the 1974 Daytona 200. Late in his career, he rode for Yamaha, proving his ability to ride the hairy Yamaha TZ 750, as well as the smooth MVs.**

its works machines were some beautiful little 125cc production racers. These were single-cylinder machines, with a gear-driven overhead cam. They were not as fast as the twin-cam works versions but were effective mounts for amateur racers.

Domenico died in 1971. Finally, in the early seventies, MV released the 750cc America, but it came too late and couldn't match the Japanese bikes in quality. The America struck many potential buyers as a cheap attempt to cash in on MV's famous name. Not long after this unsuccessful

foray into production superbikes, MV withdrew from motorcycle manufacturing altogether.

MV Agusta's works racers gathered dust in a corner of the helicopter factory until the eighties, when most were sold to the New York–based Team Obsolete vintage racing squad. A few were subsequently resold to other well-heeled collectors. Considering MV's racing success, almost every one of these museum pieces has a Grand Prix history. Ruggero Mazza has undertaken the restoration of several, but it seems unlikely that these bikes will change hands again, except at

months to complete the detailed design and manufacturing of this mechanical marvel. The carburetors were adjusted by running the engine in a darkened room and watching the color of the eight tiny exhausts as they glowed red hot.

The finished motorcycle weighed about 325 pounds (147.5kg), a weight that was scarcely more than a Manx Norton and was the result of a fanatical obsession with weight savings. The frame was unpainted to save the weight of the paint. Guzzi's stylish "dustbin" fairing was an avocado color because that happened to be the available color of corrosion-resistant primer; to save more weight, the fairing also had to do without a final gloss coat.

Unfortunately, the desire for low weight compromised chassis stiffness, suspension, and tires. The net result was a motorcycle that crashed on its first shakedown run and had an evil will of its own. Bill Lomas, who won two 350cc world championships on Moto Guzzis, rode the 500, too. He diplomatically recalled, "The V8 riders all had very hair-raising moments." While the machine had speed, its reliability and handling problems prevented it from earning a victory.

Perhaps frustrated by the cost of developing the V8 and the comparative lack of results, Moto Guzzi withdrew from Grands Prix in 1957. Fortunately, two or three of these amazing motorcycles survived, and another has since been built up from a mixture of spare and replica parts. Thus, vintage racing fans do occasionally still hear the 12,000-rpm howl of this engine, which represents the very end of its evolutionary line.

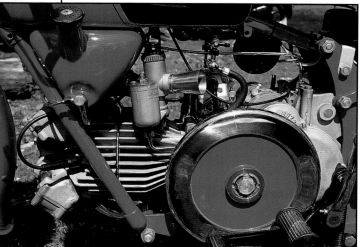

Above: **Moto Guzzi "California" 1100cc. The perils of trying to out-Harley Harley-Davidson are evident.** *Left:* **500cc horizontal single cylinder engine from a Moto Guzzi Falcone. This engine was produced for forty years. Note large external flywheel.** *Opposite:* **The Indian Sales Company equipped this Indian-badged Royal Enfield for duty with the New York City Police Department, c.1955. Many government agencies specified that equipment be "American made," and in Indian's final days the last Chiefs, along with some of these British twins, were sold for this purpose.**

prices more conveniently expressed in fractions of a million.

Undaunted by MV Agusta's huge effort, Moto Guzzi and Gilera both contributed to spirited competition through the mid-fifties. Moto Guzzi was by far the most established Italian manufacturer, and under intense design pressure from these two upstarts, Guzzi responded in 1954 with the creation of a unique oddity in the history of Grand Prix racing: a 500cc V8.

Guzzi's V8 was a response to the axiom that, beyond a certain point, increased power can come only from higher revs. Higher revs, in turn, are limited by factors like piston speed and mass. The same equations would later force Honda to field five- and six-cylinder machines. MV went from three cylinders to four, and experimented with a Six before noise limitations and other rules limited the largest Grand Prix class to four-cylinder two-strokes.

Giulio Carcano sketched the V8 on a napkin, while the Guzzi team ate in a restaurant after the 1954 Spanish Grand Prix. Guzzi's small, eleven-man racing department then took only a few

The Continent Takes the Lead

Of all the motorcycle brands in the world, only BMW can legitimately challenge Harley-Davidson as the single most recognizable marque. There's no doubt that a good portion of both manufacturers' brand awareness can be credited to their steadfast reliance on distinctive engine layouts. Fashions come and go, but Harley-Davidson has offered little but longitudinal V-twins since 1911. Starting only a decade later, BMW has made the transverse-mounted flat twin their choice for more than seventy-five years.

In recent years, the Japanese manufacturers have built V-twins, which are little more than Harley knockoffs. None have dared to challenge BMW's hegemony over the flat twin, however; perhaps they still fear inevitable comparison to the quality of the Bavarian marque.

It was not always so. Indeed, BMW was not the first to build a flat twin, nor were they the only company to popularize the design.

The ABC motorcycle was designed by Englishman Granville Bradshaw and produced in fits and starts from 1914. It got its name

Below: **1967 BMW R60/2. BMW reverted to "Earles" forks in the 1960s.** *Opposite:* **1939 Zundapp 750. The Wehrmacht requisitioned many of these for wartime use. Patton was impressed with the performance of such shaft-driven opposed twin motorcycles during the desert war, and had Harley-Davidson build 1,000 similar prototypes, which were called "XA"s (for "experimental army"). While the Zundapp had a good reputation, Harley chose to copy the superb BMW R75.**

from the All British Engine Company, Bradshaw's employer. Production of the motorcycle reached its peak in 1919–1921, when it was being manufactured by Sopwith, of World War I aircraft fame. While it offered many technological advances in its day, the Sopwith/ABC was released with insufficient development, and the rash of warranty claims forced Sopwith into liquidation in 1921. The timing of the development of the Sopwith/ABC and the aircraft manufacturing connection to BMW suggest that Bradshaw's design may have inspired BMW's engineers.

The Aristos was another innovative German flat twin produced in 1923 and 1924. While BMW took advantage of the flat-twin cylinders' free access to passing airflow for cooling, the Aristos and subsequent Menos and Sterna brands relied on water cooling. Their welded sheet metal "monocoque" chassis, with radiator mounted low on the side, seemed to predict the modern F1 racing car. Astra was another German manufacturer building a flat-twin powered motorcycle at the same time. Astras were the first preferred mount of the record-seeking Ernst Henne. In 1937, having switched to BMWs, Henne rode a supercharged 500, attaining a speed of 173 miles per hour (278kph)!

Shortly after World War II, a former aircraft factory in Italy began producing Capriolo motorcycles, including a 149cc flat twin in a pressed-steel frame similar to those in use by Honda at the same time.

Of course, to the victors went the spoils of war, and CMR in France began selling motorcycles assembled out of BMW parts in 1945. A few years later, the company was renamed Cemec and began

producing BMW knockoffs, which were sold until 1955. After that, the French factory began producing a line of French-designed flat twins called Ratiers, with 500 and 600cc displacements.

When Germany was partitioned after WWII, the former DKW works at Zschopau became the state-owned IFA factory. (Later, it would come to be known as Motorradwerke Zschopau, or MZ.) Here, a 350cc two-stroke flat twin was produced, which bore a certain cosmetic similarity to a BMW, though offering only 15 horsepower. Much later, in the early seventies, a Russian state-owned company sold the Cossack Ural, an imitation BMW R65 that was also mildly tuned, to produce only about 30 horsepower.

Universal, the maker of Swiss Helvetia motorcycles from 1928 to 1964, produced a 578cc flat twin with shaft drive, as well as a shaft-drive 250cc single in the mid-fifties. Notwithstanding the overt similarities to models from the BMW line, the Swiss designed their own engines from clean sheets of paper. Condor, another of Switzerland's most respected manufacturers, made a sturdy-looking 678cc flat twin at this time.

Douglas, an English manufacturer, came closest to usurping BMW's "ownership" of the flat twin. J.F. Barter, Douglas' designer, had a head start, first hanging a longitudinally mounted flat-twin engine underneath a bicycle crossbar in 1907. It took a while to get the layout right, and in the late twenties, Douglases appeared with low-mounted in-line flat twins of 350cc displacement. In the thirties, transverse-mounted 500cc twins were produced with shaft drives,

and after World War II Douglas stuck with this layout exclusively. The company ceased production in 1956, with the 350cc Dragonfly as its crowning achievement.

From the mid-thirties through 1950, the venerable German firm of Zundapp produced a range of flat twins, in displacements to 750cc. They included motorcycles with innovative pressed-steel frames, though in their final evolution postwar Zundapps were sporting machines built on more conventional tubular chassis. Windhoff was another German marque that combined the transverse flat-twin

layout with a technologically advanced chassis design. Its 996cc 1929 model featured a fully stressed engine to which other chassis components were bolted.

Had the Japanese invasion of the sixties been modeled on German motorcycles instead of British ones, the Marusho gives us an idea of what motorcycling might have become. Marushos were doubtless cheaper than the BMW R50 they copied, but were unable to compete on quality despite the fact that they were built in the former Lilac works, which had produced some of Japan's most luxu-

rious motorcycles in the previous decade. The Marusho was produced only from 1965 to 1970.

Last but not least, the Hoffmann, produced in Germany during the postwar years, deserves mention. Hoffman had built Vespa scooters under license, and employed Richard Kuchen, a brilliant designer, to pen a pair of all-new 250 and 300cc designs. While the bikes were expensive and perhaps not suited to a market demanding cheap transportation, their pressed-steel frames and semienclosed design were distinctively modern in their day.

The Continent Takes the Lead

323 KNN

In Germany, NSU's biggest seller was the stylish but spartan Quickly moped. At its peak, Quickly production reached one thousand units per day, and those profits financed an effective works racing effort. NSU had been one of Germany's very first motorcycle manufacturers. The company originally made commercial knitting machines but produced its first motorcycle in 1901. Walter Moore (who designed Norton's original overhead-cam engine) designed NSU racing motorcycles before the war, but during NSU's world championship era, Walter Froede created the machines. The power output Froede achieved—about 150 horsepower

per liter of engine capacity—was impressive in their day. It was an occasion for considerable national pride in 1953 when Walter Haas became the first German to win a world championship and, to top it off, did so on a German motorcycle.

The 250cc Rennmaxes and the 125cc Rennfoxes were poised for another championship season in 1954, winning their classes at the Isle of Man. Among the spectators that year was a foreigner who was shaken by his first sight of the 125cc Rennfoxes screaming past at more than 12,000 rpm. Demoralized, he returned to his factory, realizing that his own bikes were capable of

Above: **1961 NSU Sportmax, a stylish and powerful sporting machine in its day. After NSU halted their Rennmax factory racing effort, independant tuners achieved world-class performances with this machine.** *Opposite:* **The Harley-Davidson "panhead" engine made its debut in 1949. Through the 1950s, Harley riders first "chopped" their motorcycles by stripping them of extraneous parts. By the 1960s, "choppers" had become highly individualized customs, typically with low-slung rigid frames and extended front forks. This is a replica of the chopper ridden by Peter Fonda in the movie *Easy Rider*.**

only half those speeds. That little fellow was Soichiro Honda, and he would be back.

The NSU works effort was disbanded when one of their riders was killed later that year. The factory turned its attention back to production

The Continent Takes the Lead

machines, from mopeds to 250cc lightweights. The top of their line was the Supermax, a very fine-looking motorcycle with an innovative frame; the engine was suspended from a curvaceous "spine" comprised of the steering head, gas tank, air box, and oil tank. The chain was enclosed, and the front suspension was a compact leading link design.

A Sportmax production racer was based on the Supermax, with a tuned Supermax engine and a dustbin fairing. The Sportmax, despite being based on a street machine, was competitive enough to win the 1955 world championship in the 250cc class. The "dustbins," which were huge fairings that enclosed both front wheel and rider, reduced drag by more than half and significantly impacted lap speeds on sweeping, high-speed continental tracks like Spa and Monza. In the late fifties, dustbins were banned. The reason given by the FIM was a problem with steering lock. A more likely explanation was that the British and French influence in the FIM resented the dustbins, which gave an advantage to the motorcycles produced by their old Axis enemies in Germany and Italy.

At a time when markets demanded affordable machines like the Quickly, BMW was experiencing difficulty marketing a line of motorcycles that started at more than $1,000. Early experiments with automobile production drained the firm's engineering and financial resources. Yet, perhaps luckily for motorcycling purists, the Bavarians stayed the course and continued to make detail improvements to Max Friz's classic opposed twin-cylinder design.

Friz had always been a reluctant motorcycle designer, and created the original BMW in 1923

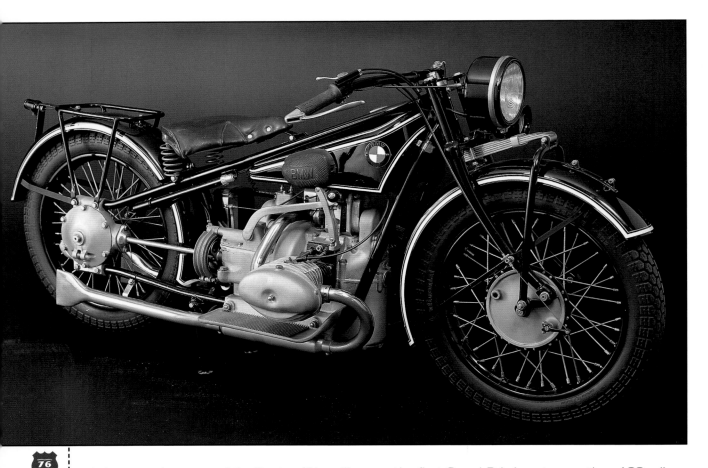

only because the terms of the Treaty of Versailles prevented BMW from building new aircraft engines. While Friz was not the inventor of the opposed twin, he recognized the merit of the "boxer" engine layout, in which the dynamic imbalance of one piston is canceled out by the other.

By 1925, an overhead-valve racing version was on track. In 1929, stylish pressed-steel frames appeared, and in 1935, BMW became the first manufacturer to use telehydraulic front forks on a production motorcycle. BMW continued this run of technological advances, with rear plunger-sprung frames in 1938 and a series of very powerful supercharged works racers.

In 1939, Walter Meier rode one of the Kompressor works racers, and was the first non-Briton ever to win the Senior TT. He also recorded the first Grand Prix lap at more than 100 miles per hour (161kph)—not bad for a Munich motorcycle cop, who after his first racing tryout protested, "Road racing is too fast and dangerous for me!" and asked to be transferred back to the off-road team, where he specialized in long, slow endurance trials.

In the aftermath of the war, BMW didn't build a new boxer twin until 1950. Factory racing efforts were hampered by the ban on supercharging, but BMW production-racing Rennsport machines were still popular with privateers. These racing machines were equipped with swing arm rear suspension and Earle's front forks.

In 1955, BMW introduced the 490cc R50 and the 590cc R69. These elegant road machines adopted the same suspension layout as the Rennsport machines, and were equipped with Earle's forks until 1969. While they were not an improvement over BMW's own earlier telehydraulic design, the Earle's were well suited to sidecar duty. The driveshaft was also enclosed within one tube of the swing arm.

The 1950s and 1960s were difficult times for BMW as a company. The transition to automobile manufacture was costly, and the company never really marketed an affordable car or motorcycle, with the exception of the peculiar Isetta three-wheeler. In 1959, only a last-minute shareholder rescue prevented a weakened BMW from being taken over by Daimler Benz. Very little development work was done on the R series, which concluded with the 42-horsepower R69S.

Even in months when it sold only a few hundred motorcycles, BMW never slackened its rigid quality control standards. Its legendary build quality, high prices, and sedate performance all contributed to the motorcycles' high survival rate. The BMWs of 1955 to 1969 are among the most reliable classics, and many still see daily use. While they are mechanically similar to newer models, the absence of a starter motor on the pre-1955 BMWs emphasizes the compact boxer layout and gives the older bikes a more athletic look. In the 1980s, BMW temporarily abandoned the boxer twin for a flat four-cylinder motor, which caused such an uproar that the company reversed its decision and brought out several new boxers to appease the purists!

Harley-Davidson, too, was having difficulties making its products conform to the demands of

The Continent Takes the Lead

the market. Since 1932, the company had a steady seller in the form of its three-wheeler Servi-Cars, which were used by police departments, post offices, and the like. Fleet sales of police motorcycles were another reliable source of revenue. As most public tenders specified "American-made," Harley was now the only possible supplier. But the auto manufacturers were aggressively chasing the cops, and the ratio of motorcycle-to-car-equipped traffic officers was falling. Something

new was needed to respond to the competition from British twins, and it came from William J. Harley, Bill Harley's son, who was now head of the venerable firm's design department.

Harley took the old KH engine, replaced the side valves with pushrods, and designed a new OHV head. This was put back into the K frame, which by then was a double cradle with front tele-scopic forks and a rear swing arm. The first of the famous Sportsters, the XL, reached the market in 1957 and immediately began selling at twice the rate of the KH.

All early Sportsters were 883cc (the choice of engine displacement was based on insurance rates, which increased for bikes over 900cc). In 1958, the XLH was introduced, with high-com-pression heads and larger valves, and later that year a speed-tuned "scrambler" hit the market,

dubbed the XLCH. The XLCH adopted the Harley-Davidson "peanut" fuel tank, which had previously shown up on racing machines. Originally, it was also equipped with a two-into-one high-mounted exhaust, but even Harley-Davidson quickly realized no one was going to scramble a motorcycle that weighed more than 450 pounds (204kg). A pair of staggered, low-mounted twin pipes followed. With the small tank, the visual effect was hand-some and minimal.

While the handling of the Sportster prevented it from hounding the best British bikes through the bends, it didn't lack for speed. North America, after all, is the land of "go on green," and the Sportster's straightline performance, along with a bulletproof clutch and gearbox, provided a built-in-the-U.S.A. option to Americans feeling the need for speed.

Opposite: **Max Friz's initial design for the BMW is still clearly recognizable, seventy-five years later. This early model (c.1925) shows the faithful copy of Indian's trademark front forks.** *Right:* **Harley-Davidson's 883cc XLH engine.** *Below:* **1959 Harley-Davidson XLH Sportster. While it no doubt contributes to rider comfort, the windscreen on this Sportster is not in keeping with its minimal-ist aesthetic. Sales of this model immediately doubled those of the KH, which it replaced. (The KH had been sold as a "woman's Harley" because it was easy to kick start!)**

Chapter

6

The
Japanese
Infiltration

Between 1950 and 1960, the Japanese motorcycle industry consolidated from fifty manufacturers to four. Entering the sixties, Honda was the clear leader, with sales of the Honda Supercub making it the most popular motorcycle in the world, even before it had become available in Europe or America.

Honda's early results in Grand Prix competition piqued the Europeans' curiosity, and in 1960 Hondas began showing up at motorcycle shows and at dealers. Initially, the emphasis was on Supercubs, and it took some time before self-styled "experts" believed that the bike's 49cc engine, which redlined at 9500 rpm, would survive the rigors of regular commuting.

The skepticism of the "real motorcycle" community, however, was of little concern to the buyers of Supercubs, as they did not think of themselves as motorcyclists at all. Honda's Cub design was already ten years old, but the design brief it had filled in postwar Japan was still relevant.

Supercubs were lightweight, easy-to-handle, reliable transportation. The step-through design appealed to women. The enclosed chain and engine were tidy and a visual reminder of the bike's minimal maintenance requirements. The pressed-steel spine frame and plastic fairing ensured that it didn't even really look like a motorcycle, which was fine by Honda. They set out to redefine motorcycling as something fun, clean, and wholesome, epitomized by the marketing slogan, "You meet the nicest people on a Honda."

Traditional motorcycle manufacturers, who had previously been baffled by scooters, were again struck dumb. "We don't make much money on little bikes," they seemed to reason. "Let them have that market if they want it." Following in Piaggio's footsteps, Honda quickly turned this new category into a profitable market niche.

In Britain, especially, the big bike companies were blinkered to anything but the U.S. export market, which provided most of their profit. Little did Triumph or Norton realize that, soon enough, Honda would have full-size motorcycles to offer, too. And to boot, by the time the big bikes arrived, the Japanese had brainwashed motorcyclists out of long-accepted beliefs, for example, that all motorcycles leak oil.

The first full-size Honda to be sold in quantity in the West was the 305cc Dream. Like the Supercub, the Dream was a top-selling model in Japan long before it was exported. The design was introduced in 1953, when leading link forks were still the rage. The Dream retained the dated forks and Honda's signature pressed-steel spine frame. This time, Honda's competitors reassured themselves that the "funny" engine displacement of 305cc was just an overbored 250, and was an indication that Honda had no intention of marketing outside the Lightweight category.

Nonetheless, Honda wanted a credible street machine for the hardcore motorcyclist. The CB77 was a speed-tuned version of the Dream engine, mounted in a somewhat more traditional frame of welded tubing. It was equipped with up-to-date-looking telescopic forks, and while its handling was

You meet the nicest people on a Honda. Almost anyone can handle it. Prices start about $215*. Insurance is a drop in the bucket. And upkeep inconsequential. The persistent 4-stroke OHV engine coaxes 200 miles from a gallon of gas. So you can run around all day long. For peanuts. Clearly, the world's biggest seller. HONDA

Pages 78–79: **1964 Honda RC 165. Determined to make their four-stroke engines competitive with Yamaha's two-strokes, Honda produced a handful of miniature multis, including a five-cylinder 125, and this 250 cc transverse six. In the mid-1960's Honda were already a dominant force on the track, but their revenues were still overwhelmingly dependant on "Cub" runabouts.** *Top:* **1963 Honda CA77 Dream, 305 cc. This was the largest Honda of its day. A sports version, the "Benly" offered deceptive speed.** *Left:* **Honda's advertising emphasized their user-friendly designs, making the idea of motorcycling less threatening to neophytes.** *Opposite:* **The Ariel Leader was one of the few successful counterattacks by motorcycling's "old guard." It was reliable, practical, and still capable of sporting performance. Removable liners, with handles for use as shopping bags, fit the panniers.**

The Japanese Infiltration

no threat to the British 500s, it was infinitely more reliable and good for a legitimate 100 miles per hour (161kph). As a practical road bike with sporting performance, it was another warning that went unheeded.

All this is not to say that British manufacturers completely failed to respond to Honda's infringement (and Piaggio's, for that matter) on their territory. In 1958, one of the most interesting footnotes in the Ariel story was about to be written as the company introduced the Ariel Leader.

After almost sixty years of building motorcycles, Ariel was finally into its last decade. By then it was the runt of the BSA litter, dominated by

The Japanese Infiltration

coherent answer to the plea for progression along civilized lines."

The fuel tank was located in the pressed-steel frame, under the seat, which kept the center of gravity low. What looked like a fuel tank, between the seat and handlebars, was actually a useful "glove compartment." Rigid panniers had pullout liners with carry straps and doubled as shopping bags. There was even a clock on the instrument panel.

In short order, Ariel released the Arrow and a sports version, with the same basic frame, less bodywork, and an exposed engine. There was even a trials version, which Sammy Miller rode in a well-publicized attempt to scale Ben Nevis, the highest peak in Great Britain.

British motorcycle registrations peaked in 1959 and then entered a long recession. The Austin Seven, Morris Minor, and Mini finally became affordable as bank interest rates fell and government disincentives were relaxed.

Triumph. In 1959, the last Ariel four-strokes were killed off, including the sporting Red Hunter singles and the Square Four, which by then had grown to 1,000cc.

Val Page was left at Ariel, where he designed an interesting 50cc four-stroke he called the Pixie. It would have provided the Honda Supercub with competition, but was shelved when BSA management decided that the new engine would be too costly to develop. Page was ordered to create a new Ariel around an existing BSA 250cc two-stroke motor.

Minimal cost was essential if the design was to actually see production, so Page opted for pressed-steel construction. Even the trailing link front forks were stamped. The engine was fully enclosed, as was the chain. The rider was protected from wind and dirt by leg shields and footboards. (The footboards also helped shield the pressed-steel chassis from the British climate, where rust was endemic. This was the one flaw with the pressed frame: compared to tubing the

wall thicknesses were less, and the surface area was greater, making corrosion problematic.)

The Leader was a success, and British consumers evidently believed Ariel's marketing claim that it was "Tomorrow's motorcycle today!" Page incorporated a number of clever features that prompted Motor Cycle to extol, "Never before has a motorcycle provided a more complete and

The Japanese Infiltration

Above: **Dick Mann. Many American racers preferred wide dirt track–style handlebars on road courses, too.** *Right:* **1967 Cheney-framed Triumph. Triumph sold scramblers of their own, but the powerful Bonneville engine also found its way into specials like this one.** *Opposite, top:* **The Ariel Square Four lasted nearly thirty years. Later models had four exhaust headers to help strip heat away from rear cylinders' exhaust ports.** *Opposite, bottom:* **The smallest Norton, a 1961 Jubilee model, 250cc. The enclosed chain and deeply valenced fenders are a concession to the popularity of the Leader, Vespa, and Dream.**

If the British manufacturers (excepting Ariel) didn't seem to notice Honda's infiltration of the European market in the early sixties, it is perhaps because they were busy pouring new bikes into the American market, which had a growing appetite for top-of-the-line sports machines. Even American dirt-track racing, once the exclusive province of Harley-Davidson, was being used as a way to promote British steel. In 1963, Dick Mann rode a Matchless G50 in dirt-track events, and a BSA Gold Star on pavement to win the AMA Grand National Championship.

In the booming desert-racing scene of Southern California, British twins ruled. Johnson Motors, which distributed Triumph motorcycles in the western United States, had a catalog of custom parts that could be used to "hop up" the

In 1954, Soichiro Honda visited the Isle of Man for the TT races. As Honda made only small motorcycles, it was the Ultra-Lightweight TT that he was most interested in watching. That year, the NSU Rennfoxes were dominant, with Austrian ace Rupert Hollous taking the win.

Honda was curious but polite, and kept to the company of a few of his employees. In the best of times, the British have a ubiquitous disdain of things foreign, to which was added an extra helping of postwar xenophobia. Who could forget the fall of Singapore? It is easy to imagine muttered comments of "Oo's the wog?" and "Cor, intha' a fookin Jap, then?"

To add injury to insult, Honda left the Island demoralized by the Rennfoxes, which were generating twice the horsepower of his best engines. Most competitors at the Island thought they'd seen the last of Honda. But they didn't know him. The rise of the world's greatest motorcycle company can be fully attributed to the fierce willpower and individuality of one Soichiro Honda.

He was a blacksmith's son. Before the war he apprenticed as a mechanic, then returned to his small town where he set up a shop and worked on the few local cars that existed. He loved to race, but his wife convinced him to give it up when he was hurt in a crash. As a mechanic, Honda realized his horizons were limited. "No one," he said, "will ever bring their car from America or Europe to have it serviced in my shop."

In 1937, Honda formed a company to make piston rings. He worked doggedly, even sleeping in the factory, but couldn't solve a quality-control problem that saw his rings break up soon after they were installed in any engine. One of his friends convinced him that no mat-

Above: **Honda's first motorcycle, the 100cc two-stroke "Dream Type D," 1950.** *Below:* **Soichiro Honda straddles a 1959 Honda RC 160, 250cc. (Photo taken in 1990)** *Opposite, above:* **The Isle of Man, 1961. Mike Hailwood (right) won in both 125cc and 250cc classes. Other riders: Luigi Taveri, center; Tom Phillis, left.** *Opposite, below:* **1966 Honda RC166. The famous six-cylinder 250. Jim Redman and Mike Hailwood rode these, with Mike taking the Championship. Imagine Nobby Clark pushing you off down the pit lane with the admonition "Keep it under 20,000 RPM"!**

ter how hard he worked, his company would never succeed until his product was of acceptable quality.

Honda turned to the staff of the Hamamatsu Technical School for advice and was told that the problem with his rings was likely raw material with too little silicon. Honda later admitted, "I was ashamed that I not only failed to appreciate the need for silicon in the alloy, I didn't even know what silicon was!"

The staff at the school convinced Honda to sign on as a student, but he stubbornly refused to take notes or even attend classes that did not relate directly to piston rings. His professor told him that without a change in his attitude, he would never graduate. Honda retorted, "A ticket will get you into a movie, but a diploma will not get you a job!"

Despite his very un-Japanese attitude toward authority, Honda's piston rings were of superior quality by 1939, and he had a lucrative contract supplying Toyota. Unfortunately, the factory was bombed during the war, and the parts that remained standing were leveled soon after in an earthquake.

By 1948, Honda was already forty years old, and started over from scratch. Without family connections or a prestigious degree, Japanese banks were not interested in lending him money. MITI, the powerful Japanese Ministry of International Trade and Industry, treated him like a pariah. Nonetheless, Honda identified a pressing need for basic transportation. He purchased several hundred war surplus motors (they were intended for small generators) and modified them for

attachment to bicycles. Gas was in very short supply in postwar Japan. Cleverly, Honda tuned his engines to run on a mixture of turpentine and gasoline, and also sold the fuel mixture.

Originally, Honda intended his new company to be a supplier of customer engines. When his key distributors told him they couldn't absorb any more motors, he decided to build a complete motorbike. In 1949, the first Honda Dream Type-D was released. It had a 100cc two-stroke engine of Honda's own design. Soon, Honda's seventy employees were producing about one hundred cycles a month. Initial sales gave rise to optimism, but it became apparent that quieter, less-smoky four-stroke engines were destined to be more popular.

In 1949, Honda was still an outsider to the powerful "Zaibatsu" business groups, which colluded to promote each others' interests. He had to find private investors to fund a four-stroke development program. Within a couple of years, Honda's new motor was the best of its kind in Japan. Again, Honda envisioned himself a supplier of customer engines, and the first of the new four-strokes went to the Kitagawa Motorcycle Company. Honda opted to build an entire motorbike only

when, once again, his main customer protested that they couldn't use as many motors as the Honda factory could produce.

The motorcycle Honda built was the step-through Cub model, with an automatic transmission and a pressed-steel chassis. It had been designed for ease of use by nonmotorcyclists and paid particular attention to the needs of female riders. It was perhaps the most astute model introduction in the history of motorcycling, and sales of the Cub and its follow-up, Supercub, staggered the Japanese industrialists who had so recently spurned the crude blacksmith's son.

After visiting the Isle of Man in 1954, Honda entered a team in

the All-Japan Motorcycle Endurance Road Races, with somewhat disappointing results, between 1955 and 1957. Demoralized again, Honda vowed, "We should never imitate foreign technology. We must win through our own, no matter how hard it is to develop." Honda's racing department took his instructions to heart—the list of Honda innovations began soon afterward and has not yet stopped.

Honda returned to the Isle of Man in 1959, when his team of three much-improved 125cc racers ran reliably. Four midpack finishes were enough to earn Honda the Manufacturer's Prize in the class. While most were still skeptical, a few British journalists patrolled Honda's large, well-organized pits and warned local fans to expect more from the Japanese in years to come.

In 1960, Honda brought complicated four-cylinder 250cc racers and had a best finish of fourth place. The Honda dynasty began in 1961, when a young Mike Hailwood won both the Ultra-Lightweight and Lightweight TTs, and Hondas also finished second, third, fourth, and fifth in both 125 and 250cc classes.

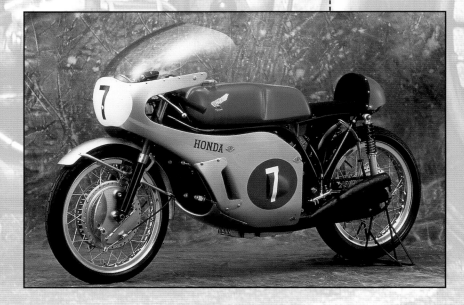

Triumph 650 twins. Demand for these parts was so great that by 1963 the factory was shipping bikes to America stripped down and ready for action in desert scrambles.

Versions of the Bonneville and the Trophy were both shipped with knobby tires, wide handlebars, and (initially) high exhaust pipes. The Bonneville was shipped with trick engine parts, including high-lift cams, which had been developed for Triumph's land-speed-record streamliner, and was one of the most potent production motorcycles ever tested by American cycle magazines. Right from the box the Bonneville T120 TT was capable of 120 miles per hour (193kph), with sub fourteen-second/100+ mph (161kph) quarter-mile (402m) times. Originally, it was only intended for the western U.S. market, but it was snapped up by eastern drag racers, too.

Opposite: **A beautifully customized 1962 Duo-Glide.** *Above:* **Long after their unsuccessful affair with Aer Macchi, Harley-Davidson continued to flirt with manufacturers of lightweight machines. Moto Morini caught Harley's eye by making small displacement V-twins that were superficially similar to their own. After a promising courtship, Harley management failed to come to terms with Morini's widow.**

It is said that a mechanic is not needed to synchronize the Bonneville's dual Amal carburetors, but that a psychiatrist is. Despite the ferocious

The Japanese Infiltration

appeal of the Bonneville, a more practical "desert sled" for American club racers was the milder Trophy TR6SC, which had a more manageable single carb.

One of the most prestigious of the "hare and hound" races was the annual dash from Barstow, California, to Las Vegas, Nevada. Enormous dust clouds were raised in the desert as hundreds of Trophy Specials took the start in these events. Desert racing was not just popular with club racers; it was also extensively reported in cycle magazines, and was portrayed in the classic motorcycle-racing documentary film *On Any Sunday*. This sort of intensive exposure helped to cement Triumph's reputation among American sport riders.

Harley-Davidson, meanwhile, was beginning to realize that there was an awakening market for lightweight machines in the United States. They didn't trust themselves to design such a motorcycle from scratch, and so in 1960 they acquired the troubled Aer Macchi motorcycle factory, based in Milan. As the name implies, Aer Macchi (later condensed to "Aermacchi") was yet another Italian aviation firm, which began producing small motorcycles in 1948.

In Italy, Harley-Davidson produced motorcycles from 50 to 350cc. The most noteworthy were the larger 250 and 350cc single-cylinder models. These were interesting designs that betrayed the substantial talent of Aermacchi's engineers. In some, the horizontal engine hung off a pressed-steel spine, although later versions had more conventional-looking tube frames. The pushrod

engines spun at very high rpm—up to 12,000 and gave sporting performances.

These models, which Harley called Sprints, were exceptional motorcycles despite occasional quality-control problems with things like electrics and switchgear. Unfortunately, these came to light just at the time Japanese manufacturers were setting new standards in attention to such details. Furthermore, Harley-Davidson was typecast as a maker of cruising behemoths, so the Sprints didn't get a fair trial at the hands of the American motorcycling public.

Harley-Davidson used an Aermacchi to win the 250cc Daytona 100 race in 1963 and 1964.

Above: **Honda CB 450 "Black Bomber." With its introduction in 1965, Honda sought a share of the lucrative, prestigious half-liter class.** *Opposite:* **By the early 1960s, Honda could already leverage racing success into sales. The Benly was Honda's first "Super Sport" bike, with considerable appeal to young hooligans and cafe racers.**

The Japanese Infiltration

Sprints were used also successfully in half-mile (804km) dirt-track racing. Back in Europe, Aermacchi's 250 and 350 production racers were the choice of many privateer road racers.

Harley-Davidson operated Aermacchi for about twenty years. It was a relationship that never reached its potential. In the mid-seventies, however, at a time when Harley-Davidson had given up hope of actually selling lightweight motorcycles, Aermacchi's racing efforts paid off with a series of world championships in the 250 and 350cc classes.

By then, Aermacchi designers had (finally!) forgone the pushrod engine and built a modern two-stroke twin that was ridden by Walter Villa. It was capable of holding off the 250cc Yamahas and toppled the MV Agusta 350 from its throne. Unfortunately, even this achievement, which should have been one of Harley-Davidson's few bright memories from the seventies, was marked with an asterisk in the history books: the first appearance of the water-cooled AMF/Harley Davidson 250 was at Monza in 1973. It was widely reported to have seized, killing rider Renzo Pasolini as well as the brilliant Finnish world champion Jaarno Saarinen, who was directly behind Pasolini. (Pasolini's mechanics vehemently denied these reports, and it is now thought that Pasolini, Saarinen, and several others went down in oil that had leaked from a Benelli in the previous 350 race.)

In 1964, Yamaha introduced its "Autolube" oil-injection system for road-going two-strokes. Veloce had developed a similar system thirty years earlier, which freed two-stroke riders from the messy and math-intensive chore of mixing oil with their fuel. As would so often be the case, the Japanese took the idea, improved it, mass-produced it, and then mass-marketed it.

In 1965, Honda finally showed that it coveted the big-bike market. The British press, as if heralding the impending Japanese invasion, dubbed the full-size CB450 the Black Bomber. It was one of the first Honda exports that had not been tried and tested for years at home, and it is ironic that this bike, which threw the old-world manufacturers into a panic, was the closest thing to a flop from Honda.

As people expected from a new Honda, the engine was interesting. Twin overhead cams operated torsion-bar valve springs. For a bike in the 500cc class, the redline at 8500 rpm was astounding. As usual, the old guard said it would never last at those speeds, and as usual, they were wrong. It was the CB450's handling that was distinctly poorer than competing British bikes—since the bike was far too heavy, the name CB450 could have referred to the machine's weight in pounds! With rear shocks that were oversprung and underdamped as well as soft front forks, it did not encourage spirited riding.

Honda, however, had pitched the CB450 as a sports touring bike, not a full-on cafe racer. Despite its high engine speeds, it was remarkably quiet and relatively vibration-free, even cruising at more than 6000 rpm. It was not cheap, but it made significant inroads in the United States. For American long-distance highway riders, its power and reliability were attractive, and the handling was adequate. The CB450, finally, triggered responses from Triumph, BSA, and Norton, but by that time it was already too late. Hidden away in Honda's sprawling six-hundred-man Research and Development facility, work was already under way on the groundbreaking CB750-4.

Chapter

7

The
Japanese
Invasion

In the mid-sixties, Suzuki, Yamaha, and Kawasaki all followed Honda's example. First, they won a few world championships, usually in the smaller-displacement categories. Then they exported small, sporty, well-made bikes that made experienced motorcyclists think, "If they ever put out a big bike, it'll be worth a serious look."

Going into the second half of the decade, Norton, Triumph, and the others were all waiting for the other shoe to drop. The old guard knew that the Japanese manufacturers, led by Honda, were about to unleash new motorcycles in the profitable, large-displacement sports and touring categories they had previously ignored.

Harley-Davidson was caught flat-footed, with enough trouble from aggressive British importers on the U.S. home front. In Britain, Norton and BSA/Triumph found themselves in their biggest race ever—the race to build and market the next generation of street motorcycles. The rules of engagement were well understood: the coming generation of Japanese engines were sure to be more powerful, more reliable, and smoother than anything yet seen.

Norton had been planning to design an all-new 800cc twin engine, which it had code-named the Z26. But development capital for a new engine was impossible to find, as Norton's parent company, AMC, was on the brink of bankruptcy. Norton's assets were acquired by Manganese Bronze Holdings, which had taken control of Villiers, a company that manufactured small engines. MBH amalgamated the two firms, creating a new company called Norton-Villiers.

Without the money for a new motor, there seemed little to do but bore out the old Atlas

engine, which was quickly done. To no one's surprise, it proved prone to spectacular crankshaft failures and rider-numbing vibration. There was little to do about the cranks; they simply required more precision in assembly than Villiers could provide. Nor was there a means of balancing the engine, with its 360-degree crank and outdated "long-stroke" dimensions.

Norton, however, did come up with a clever means of minimizing the vibrations. By bolting the swing arm to a separate, rubber-mounted subframe containing the engine, the rest of the chassis, including the rider, was isolated from most of the shaking. This new frame was dubbed "isolastic." It serves to illustrate both the best and worst aspects of the moribund British motorcycle industry. At its best, the isolastic frame was an inge-

nious end-run around a problem, with the result that the new Norton retained the famous Norton handling. At its worst, the frame was a cobbled-together solution to a problem that should have been addressed years sooner with an all-new engine that didn't vibrate in the first place.

Ironically, Bert Hopwood, who created Norton's Atlas engine, was now head of design for both BSA and Triumph. Triumph's American dealers wanted a 60-horsepower luxury sports-touring bike. The requested power dictated a displacement of 750cc. Hopwood had seen his Atlas engine bored to 750cc, and knew that it shook too much and would self-destruct if tuned to the requested power output. He decided to build a three-cylinder 750 with 120-degree cranks that would reduce vibration.

Initially, Hopwood intended to add a cylinder to Triumph's venerable Speed Twin engine. (This was a project Triumph designers had prototyped as early as 1963. Had they pursued it then, it would have been truly groundbreaking.) As development progressed, the bore-stroke ratio was nearly "squared," and the engine and gearbox were built as a unit. The final version still bore a strong family resemblance to the already thirty-year-old pushrod Speed Twin.

The new three-cylinder motor was to power both the Triumph Trident and the BSA Rocket 3. Edward Turner, Triumph's ex-boss, was retired but still had the ear of Britain's motorcycle journalists. He grumbled that this approach would likely not sell more bikes, insulted the intelligence of each

Above: **A 1968 Electra Glide accessorized for comfortable cruising. The next year, Harley-Davidson was taken over by American Foundry Co. (AMF), beginning the darkest period in Harley's history.** *Opposite:* **The last stronghold of the American domestic motorcycle market is challenged. A 1970 Honda 750 equipped for police duty.**

brand's supporters, and doubled the costs of marketing and spare inventories.

The two motorcycles were not identical. Triumph dropped the triple into its traditional single-downtube cradle frame, which necessitated some tricky routing of the central exhaust. It chose an awkward 3-into-2 header pipe that still looks like an afterthought. BSA, for its part, tilted the engine slightly forward in a more modern-looking double-cradle frame. The BSAs cornered a little faster, but in the United States, at least, the Triumphs sold faster.

Like the Norton Commando engine, the Trident was at best an update of an engine that was already out of date. However, the Trident did produce an honest 55 horsepower, which was very respectable at the time. Moreover, it was eminently tunable for racing. Triumph and BSA works bikes immediately made an impact at Daytona. Tridents also figured prominently in the results at the Production TT and in Formula 750, which approached the status of world championships.

The Commando had its fans, too. In September 1968, *Cycle World* waxed enthusiastic: "The Commando is simply a sports roadster that offers a sensational blend of shattering performance, well-mannered tractability, racebred handling, and fierce, sure stopping power."

The Commando was so successful that Norton-Villiers immediately killed off the rest of the Norton line in order to concentrate production on the new model. The Trident, as usual, got a head start in America, with initial production being exported immediately. British motorcyclists waited eagerly until April 1969 to get their hands on the first domestic models. For an industry that had been in recession since 1960, things looked rosy. Then Honda released the CB750.

Motorcyclists around the world gasped when they saw it. Count the exhausts! Such engines had previously been seen only on Grand Prix circuits. Horsepower has to be matched with stopping power, and the front disc brake raised those stakes, too. Unlike either the Trident or the Commando, the CB750 had an electric starter

The Japanese Invasion

and a five-speed gearbox. The horsepower claims emanating from Honda's marketing department were exaggerated, but it did have a more up-to-date overhead-cam engine: smoother, oil-tight, and infinitely more reliable than anything else on the market.

It was getting harder and harder for British manufacturers to argue that their machines out-handled the Hondas. Motorcycles were faster now, and Honda's handling problems showed up at speeds few riders dared to attempt. In the biggest market, the United States, highways were long,

straight, and smooth, placing a premium on vibration-free power. Most of all, Honda's user-friendly, reliable motorcycles quickly disabused motorcyclists of the notions that after every few hundred miles fiddly ignition tune-ups were necessary, or that each morning a small puddle of oil merely served to remind the rider that he hadn't run his machine dry.

In popular mythology, the question "What killed the British (or European, or even American) motorcycle industry?" is always answered with, "The Japanese." In fact, until the late sixties, the

Japanese motorcycle industry competed head-to-head with old-world manufacturers on the race-track, but not in the marketplace.

When it came to selling motorcycles, the Japanese preferred to create whole new categories of machine and to market them to customers beyond the reach of Norton, or Harley-Davidson for that matter. The once-vibrant British and American industries were reduced by war, recession, mismanagement, government policies, and, in the end, cheap cars. But for all that, the Honda CB750 appealed to the same riders as

Until well into the 1960s, Honda's exports of road motorcycles were mainly limited to pressed-steel models of less than 125cc. They were of high quality, but hardly bikes that stirred the blood of real motorcyclists. This was definitely not the case on the world's Grand Prix tracks, where by 1965 Honda had unveiled a series of progressively more potent machines in every class.

Especially in the area of engine development, the Japanese manufacturer (already the world's largest) seemed ever ready to raise the stakes. Even the most jaded fans were awed when Honda responded to Yamaha's two-cylinder two-strokes in 1964 with a 250cc transverse Six. Other manufacturers shuddered at rumors that the motor was developed from drawing table to asphalt in two months.

By 1965, Ralph Bryans, Luigi Taveri, Jim Redman, Tom Phillis, and others had earned world championships on Honda motorcycles from 50 to 350cc. Only the premier title—the 500cc Individual Championship—had eluded them. Looking forward to 1966, it was clear that this was Honda's foremost goal.

Yet even for Honda, the 500cc championship wouldn't be easily captured. For starters, there was MV Agusta in the way. Honda's engines were fantastic, but the company seemed to want to win on horsepower alone and had not developed its chassis as far as the Italians. This was not so much of a problem in the lighter, less powerful classes, but as the bikes got heavier and faster they were harder and harder to ride. Problems first showed up in the 250s and 350s, but the 500s were particularly bad. Anything extra the Hondas had in sheer speed was certainly needed, as the MVs were stronger under braking and able to apply power much quicker on corner exits.

Honda understood the problem, but for the first time the giant racing department was stretched thin. Efforts to build a competitive Formula

Above: **Mike Hailwood left motorcycles for car racing in the late 1960s. In 1974, he was nearly crippled in a Formula 1 car crash. His return to the Isle of Man, to win the F1 TT in 1978 was the greatest comeback in the history of motor racing.** *Below:* **Riders sprint to their motorcycles in a "Le Mans" style start, c.1976.**

I car engine were siphoning off engineering talent. Late in the 1965 season, Honda could have embarked on a costly and time-consuming chassis development program in order to build an all-new 500cc title contender. Instead, officials opted for a simpler solution: they hired Mike "the Bike" Hailwood to ride the machine they already had.

Mike Hailwood was very possibly the most gifted motorcycle racer ever. Honda was already familiar with him. In 1961, riding as a privateer (on a full "factory" bike, arranged by his father, who was England's largest motorcycle dealer), he delivered Honda its first 250cc world championship. Then from 1962 to 1965, he piloted MV Agusta 500s to world championships, denying Honda the very prize it coveted most.

Honda chose Hailwood for more than his extraordinary skill and winning record. He had a reputation as a rider who wasn't fussy. He could get on any motorcycle and ride the wheels off it, regardless of chassis gremlins. Paradoxically, it was his own smoothness on the track that allowed him to ride bikes that shook, wobbled, and slid underneath mortals. In The Art of Motorcycle Racing, he wrote, "Although it may be difficult to achieve, every rider should try, as

tidiness conserves effort. Endeavor, therefore, to develop a smooth and unobtrusive style. Aim to blend your hand, foot, and body movements into a smooth rhythm and avoid wrenching, tugging, or stamping at the controls. Violent movements achieve nothing, look flashy, and tire you out."

Honda's plan to rely on Hailwood was a good one, and at any other time in the history of motorcycle racing, it would have worked. But in 1966 and 1967, Honda could field a machine that was, at best, the equal of the MV Agusta. And the MV would be ridden by the only man who could hope to beat Hailwood on equal terms. That man was Giacomo Agostini.

Agostini didn't quite have Hailwood's physical skills—no one did—but he made up for it with a methodical approach to chassis setup that allowed him to get everything out of the bike. If Hailwood had a weakness, it was that he was too good, and was inclined to ride around problems rather than report them to his mechanics.

"Ago" had ridden as MV Agusta's "junior" team member with Mike in 1965, studying his style and learning his approach to each circuit. Mike, for his part, tried one of the six-cylinder Hondas during the 1965 Japanese Grand Prix, and reported prophetically: "To put it mildly, I have ridden machines with better handling characteristics....The engine, like all Honda motors, is a flier, however."

In 1966, Mike managed to win three 500cc Grands Prix, which (combined with Jim Redman's results) earned Honda enough points for the Manufacturer's Trophy, but Agostini took the Individual Championship. It was some consolation for Honda that Hailwood won the titles in both the 250 and 350cc classes. In 1967, Mike won five 500cc races, but Agostini again took the championship in the big class.

Nobby Clark, Mike's mechanic at the time, said later, "In '66 and '67, it was Mike winning the races, not the motorcycle." For the first time, even Hailwood couldn't make winning look easy. After each race, he climbed off the 500 with his hands raw and bleeding from the effort of keeping it on track.

Honda, perhaps in frustration, withdrew from Grand Prix racing at the end of the year. Soon after, Mike Hailwood retired from motorcycle competition to pursue a career in Grand Prix car racing. Agostini continued the most successful motorcycle racing career in history, eventually winning 122 Grands Prix.

There has never been another rivalry to compare to Hailwood vs. Agostini. They were the first superstar motorcycle racers, media darlings in the sixties' "Jet Set." Debate still rages between English and Italian fans as to which one of these two was really the best ever.

the Trident or Commando and dealt a heavy blow to the weakened British industry. It was also one of the first bikes to really challenge Harley's hegemony in the heavy-cruiser segment of the American market. Harley must have shuddered when the California Highway Patrol quickly outfitted a CB750 for testing as a fleet bike.

If the Honda CB750 was awesome, Kawasaki's 500cc two-stroke Mach III was simply outrageous. At 60 horsepower and 400 pounds (181.5kg), even professional racers approached it with caution. In magazine tests, Mach IIIs recorded quarter-mile (402m) times that were previously reserved for full-on drag bikes. In terms of sheer acceleration, which had always been closest to American riders' hearts, the Mach III was the hottest motorcycle ever to hit the pavement.

Hitting the pavement, in fact, was a very real possibility if the Kawasaki's formidable acceleration brought a corner up too quickly. Brakes and

Below: **Cal Rayborn after winning the 1968 Daytona 200, on the only Harley-Davidson to finish the race.** *Above, right:* **1969 Kawasaki Mach III. Even professional racers approached it with caution.**

chassis were nowhere near capable of taming the engine's output. A front disc was fitted later on, and after the first two or three years, Kawasaki detuned the Mach III.

Kawasaki referred to the Mach III engine as the H1. These engines immediately attracted the attention of racers, and one surmises that many were available, since they were taken out of crashed street bikes! It wasn't long before Kawasaki itself built a production racer, which it called the H1R. Flaws on the street—noise, smoke, and only 18 miles per gallon (29km per 3.8L) of fuel—were immaterial on the track. The chassis, brakes, and suspension of the racer were up to the task. As the sixties closed, this was a rare gift from Kawasaki to privateers: a motorcycle that, if you had the talent and guts, could be purchased from the importer and put squarely on the grid of a 500cc Grand Prix. Ginger Molloy used one in 1970 to chase Agostini all the way to

the 500cc title. Racing Kawasakis were all the same color, and they figured so prominently on track that the shade is still immediately recognizable to motorcyclists as "Kawasaki green."

Kawasaki had been building lightweight two-strokes since immediately after the war. In the mid-sixties, they took over Meguro, an established Japanese motorcycle manufacturer, and continued to produce Meguro's copy of BSA's A10 650 twin. Kawasaki had better things in mind. Although always the smallest of the Japanese "Big Four," Kawasaki has introduced more than its fair share of innovative designs. To create brand awareness in the United States, it needed something capable of immediate impact. Kawasaki used the Mach III to buy time. Back in Japan, it had the defining motorcycle of the seventies on the drawing board.

The 1969 model year introduced the Honda CB750, Kawasaki Mach III, Triumph Trident, and Norton Commando. It was a watershed year for developments overseas, and was noteworthy for the passing of another institution stateside. At the end of 1968, under pressure from importers, the AMA dropped the rule limiting overhead-valve racing engines to 500cc. Effectively, this rang the death knell for Harley's 750cc side-valve KR production racer.

With other manufacturers' 750s now eligible for competition, Harley-Davidson immediately realized they would have to develop an overhead-valve 750 of their own. In fact, it had long been ironic that the only side-valve motorcycles in Harley's catalog were the racing bikes. Born in 1952, the KR was so dated that had it been a rider, it would have been old enough for a pro license!

In fact, it was doubtful that the "extra" 250cc allowed to Harley's side-valve engines under the old rules even constituted an advantage. They were already forced to push the KRTT to the very limit on road courses. In 1968, Harley entered seven bikes in the Daytona 200; six failed to finish. They must have held their breath as Cal Rayborn, in the last one, crossed the line to win.

Over their eighteen-year term as Harley's works racers, about 500 KRs were given to factory riders and sold to privateers. These were ridden to thirteen AMA championships. KR-mounted racers scored countless victories on half-mile (804m) and mile (1.6km) ovals, on road courses, and on TT tracks. (In the United States, "TT" circuits are dirt, with both right and left turns, and jumps.)

The KR was unique among racing motorcycles in that the whole rear of the motorcycle was a detachable subframe, so that it could be raced

Successor to the KR, Harley's XR was introduced in 1969. It has ruled the dirt tracks of America for nearly thirty years.

---

with a rigid frame on dirt tracks, and a swing arm rear suspension on road courses. With its compact engine and spartan frame, the KR is the classic American production racer, and modern mechanics are still impressed that "good old boy" tuners like Tom Sifton managed to extract so much power, for so long, from the primitive motor.

The KR was ultimately replaced by another elegant racer, the XR, but teething troubles prevented it from being ready for the 1969 season opener, so Cal Rayborn raced—and won in—the KR one last time at Daytona. Harley was never again competitive there, and the win testified to Rayborn's extraordinary skill. Cal Rayborn was later killed while racing in New Zealand.

Rayborn rarely raced against the best European riders, but in occasional Transatlantic Challenge races, he proved that he could show any of them the way home. When *Cycle* magazine named him Rider of the Year in 1973, they bragged that he "... made it clear the FIM's 'World Champions' really are European champions, no matter what the trophies say." Cal and the KR he rode epitomized the best in American motorcycle racing: unpretentious, but ready to race on any track, any surface, anywhere, and give it everything he had.

Chapter 8

Early Superbikes

Triumph and Norton weren't the only ones caught short by the unveiling of the Honda 750 in 1968. Kawasaki had been about to release its own across-the-frame, four-cylinder motorcycle, which they dubbed the Z1. Once they realized Honda had stolen the march, however, Kawasaki delayed the launch of the Z1, handing its engineers a new CB750 and the firm instructions to "top this."

Within a couple of years, Kawasaki's Research and Development Department had a working prototype. Its engine displaced 903cc, and featured chain-driven twin overhead cams. Rumors placed its top speed at 140 miles per hour (225kph). Other manufacturers scoffed that it was impossible; but they were just whistling past the graveyard.

Motorcycles over 750cc were illegal in seismic-prone Japan. In 1972, Kawasaki took one of the prototypes, disguised as a Honda, to the United States for an extended road test. The code name for this development machine was "New York Steak"; the catchy moniker suggests that Kawasaki's marketing department was already conducting a prelaunch campaign of press "leaks." The next round of prototypes went to Daytona, where they were ridden by Paul Smart and Yvon DuHamel in a private test. Both seasoned pros were shaken by the prototype's earthshattering speed. It had been "tweaked" in the factory racing shop, but it was still essentially a street motorcycle, and it went 145 miles an hour (233kph). On top of that, it was durable enough to set twenty-four-hour endurance records.

The Kawasaki Z1 was available early in the 1973 model year. If it had any more macho appeal, it would have come from the factory covered in hair, not paint or chrome. Twenty-five years earlier, Gilera proved the merit of the four-cylinder engine on their Grand Prix bikes. Five years after Honda established the viability of its mass production, Kawasaki perfected it and delivered the first modern superbike. Even *Motorcycle News* readers voted it Machine of the Year over their beloved home-grown Commando.

The Z1 was a strong seller, and Kawasaki built up to five thousand of them per month. Its subsequent model, the slightly milder Z900, was produced only until 1976, but the Z1's influence is still visible in current Kawasakis.

If you survey the grid of a modern World Superbike Championship race, most of the spots will be filled with bikes that trace their engines back to the Z1. But if Ducati's current dominance of WSB runs true to form, the front row will be filled with slim Italian twins, not tire-burning Japanese Fours. The heritage of current racing Ducatis is evident at a glance. They directly follow the line established by the Ducati 750 Imola, which was introduced in 1972.

Ducati got a comparatively late start in the Italian motorcycle industry and did not build their first bikes until 1950. In short order, however, designer Fabio Taglione was up to speed. By the mid-sixties, the 250cc Mach 1 was by far the fastest street bike in its class.

By then, Taglione was already building Ducati works racers with "desmodromic" valves. The desmo system had been used in Azzariti motorcycles briefly in the thirties, but it was left to Ducati to perfect its manufacture. Basically, this system uses a cam to open the valves, as usual, but also uses another cam (instead of springs) to close them. This eliminates valve float at high rpm and prevents the valves from contacting the pistons under racing conditions. Ducati's innovative desmodromic 125cc racers could spin to 15,000 rpm, and the bikes quickly proved their merit in Grand Prix racing.

In 1971, the desmo valve gear found its way onto Ducati street bikes, which were mostly big singles, up to 450cc. Two of these singles were mated into a 90-degree V-twin, which displaced 750cc. This was a fine design, which tilted the "V" forward until the front cylinder was almost horizontal, and allowed both air-cooled cylinders to bathe in a flow of fresh air. The chassis was an open-cradle design that used the engine casing as a stressed member, and was equally advanced for its time.

Rule changes that had recently been instituted by the American Motorcycle Association sparked a growing interest in "production-based"

Pages 100-101: **1972 Honda CB 500 Four. Honda followed the success of their 750 with a series of progressively smaller four-cylinder models.** *Opposite, top:* **1974 Yamaha RD 250. The RD stood for "Race Developed," and the performance of these brilliant two-strokes justified the initals.** *Opposite, bottom:* **A 750cc T140 "Silver Jubilee" Bonneville from 1977.** *Above:* **The term "Super-bike" was coined in the late 1960s to describe any motorcycle capable of covering a quarter mile in under 14 seconds, reaching a speed of over 90 mph (145kph). There were a number of motorcycles dubbed Superbike before the Kawasaki Z1, but all bowed to the "Z" when it appeared in 1973. The four-into-one exhaust on this machine is not original.**

Formula 750 racing. Unlike Grand Prix motorcycles (especially in the premiere 500cc class), Formula 750 motorcycles resembled the bikes that fans rode on the street, and fan interest was very high. Formula 750 evolved into the present-day AMA World Superbike Championships and the FIM World Superbike Championship.

The Europeans, having been to the Daytona 200, realized that large crowds and extensive publicity could be attracted with a comparable event on the Continent. The first Imola 200 was held in 1972. The promoters put up a purse and appearance money that attracted the top riders of the day, and many factories supplied works bikes that, at least in theory, were based on 750cc street machines.

Early Superbikes

Ducati built up a pair of its new 750cc V-twins with desmo valves, and contracted Paul Smart and Bruno Spaggiari as riders. Initially, they were unfamiliar with the motorcycles and had low expectations. MV Augusta had prepared one of its 750cc shaft-drive street machines for the great Agostini. Ago found the MV completely unmanageable in practice, while Smart and Spaggiari quickly realized that they were on absolutely dominant machinery. The night before the event, since it

was certain one of them would win, they agreed to split the prize.

During the race, the two Ducati riders distanced themselves from the field, and even Ago could not mount a challenge. Smart and Spaggiari rode in formation much of the race, and with a few laps to go, the Ducati pit gave each rider permission to go for the win. Smart took it, with Spaggiari in his slipstream.

Everyone was suddenly talking about Ducati's desmo twin, and it was not long before the factory released a limited number of street versions with desmodromic valve gear. The Ducati Imola 750 was thus the first of a line that is still winning superbike races twenty-five years later. Then, as now, Ducati twins were bikes aimed at real aficionados who wanted a factory-built "special" to ride on the road. They were priced accordingly; $2,500 was a lot of money for any motorcycle, and the price prompted *Cycle* magazine to complain that, in spite of a superb engine and brilliant handling, "The factory is no better at doing specials than most enthusiasts when it comes to tanks, seats, and bars. Clearly, those are considerations about which Ducati simply doesn't care."

The same year that Ducati won at Imola, Don Emde won the Daytona 200. Don gave Yamaha its

Investing in Future Classics

Every year, motorcycle manufacturers introduce many models that they proudly describe as "instant classics." History, however, is more critical, and it is a risky business to attempt to predict future classics. BMW's K100 flat four-cylinder bike was introduced with fanfare in 1983, but never captured the imagination of the motorcycling public. When it came out, the AMF/Harley-Davidson XLCR cafe racer was spurned in the marketplace, but those machines already sell for two to three times their original price.

Despite such perils, it is tempting to try and pick a future priceless museum piece out of the Used Motorcycles section of the classifieds. So which bikes, of those released in the last decade or so, are worthy of being purchased now and placed in storage? Here are six of one and half a dozen of the other: a handful of bikes considered and rejected, and another few tipped as investments you can appreciate while they appreciate.

After the employee buyout led by Harley-Davidson's Vaughn Beals, the venerable American brand engineered an impressive turnaround in quality control. Then, in the mid-eighties, the company introduced the first really new Harley-Davidson motor in decades. This was the aluminum Evolution engine; it was aptly named, as it still bore a family resemblance to the old Knucklehead. However, about half of the four hundred or so parts in the motor were new, including quieter hydraulic lifters and cast-in iron cylinder liners, which were designed to match the heat expansion of the pistons.

The "Evo" Harleys earned back all the respect the brand had lost in the bleak days under AMF. Any of the early Evolution models will be associated with the Harley renaissance and are almost certain to have collectible status in coming decades.

Erik Buell was a Harley-Davidson engineer who played a key role in the development of the Evolution motors. He subsequently struck out on his own, building "specials" powered by speed-tuned Harley

engines. Buells, like the current Thunderbolt model, have all the properties one would associate with classics: macho, minimal styling that epitomizes the expression "form follows function," adequate power, and torque out to here. Fit and finish are superb. Buell's earliest machines were rare even when new, but he now has greater manufacturing capacity and a distribution agreement with his old employers. The only reason not to invest in one is that they are strictly an aficionado's bike, and they are all already owned by collectors who spend two hours polishing them for each hour they ride. As such, Buells are less likely to increase in value than many other motorcycles, whose significance is not already universally recognized.

Another exotic V-twin worthy of consideration is the superb Ducati F1 Replica. This was the last Ducati to be released by the original company before Ducati's takeover by the Cagiva group. It was a true race replica, selling for $7,000 in 1985 (approximately twice the cost of a new Sportster). For that price, a sufficiently talented rider

could remove the headlights, slap on some numbers, and run with the top "Battle of the Twins" race bikes. Cycle magazine said of it, "The Ducati invites spirited riding, forgiving of the novice's fluttery inputs, yet responsive to the commands of the expert." A certain classic, it nonetheless fails the investment value test. F1 Replicas will never get rarer than they are now: the two hundred that Ducati shipped to North America are already being preserved by collectors.

In 1985, Suzuki released their own race replica. It wasn't purchased by well-heeled "poseurs," but by hooligans. The bike was the RG500 Gamma, and while most have been thrashed, seized, and stuffed under guardrails, those that survive are guaranteed classics. Cycle called it "extraordinarily sensitive, in need of expert tailoring to individual riders, and potentially lethal in the hands of fools." The engine was a square-four two-stroke, which had much in common with Suzuki's RG500 Grand Prix racers. These were ridden by

Above: **Distinctive styling and awe-inspiring straight line performance made the Yamaha V-Max a hooligan's bike for the eighties. These are already being sold as "future classics."** *Left:* **Kawasaki ZX-7. For nearly thirty years, Kawasaki has done a brilliant job of releasing street machines which bear close resemblance to their factory racers.** *Far left:* **BMW R1100 RS. BMW briefly abandoned the boxer twin layout, but outraged customers convinced them to reinstate it. The R 1100 continues the BMW tradition of advanced fork design, with their own "Telever" system.** *Opposite:* **Buell S1 Lightning. Erik Buell was a young engineer who played a key role in the development of the "Evolution" engine while working for Harley-Davidson. Later, he built "Evo" engined specials, including a race bike, "Lucifer's Hammer" which had its own cult following.**

Barry Sheene to consecutive 500cc championships in 1976 and 1977, and by Marco Lucchinelli and Franco Uncini in 1981 and 1982. The Replica's performance completely outclassed other middleweights. The 600cc Kawasaki Ninja (no slouch itself!) offered 10 less horsepower, yet was fully 70 pounds (32kg) heavier.

If the Gamma was the bike most likely to bend your mind, or even break your neck, the Honda VFR750 Interceptor held down the opposite end of the sport bike scale. The Interceptor was not intended to be a racer for the street, but rather offered sport bike performance in a more stable, comfortable, tractable package. It was one of the first mass-produced motorcycles with an aluminum chassis, and the frame is a model of elegance: a pair of box-section rails plunge straight from the steering head to the swing arm pivot.

The Interceptor's best features can't be measured with a stopwatch. Over time, it becomes apparent that it is one of the few sport bikes that's comfortable around town as well as on a long journey. It is one of the best all-around street bikes ever made, destined for the sort of status that the BMW R69S has today. A definite buy.

In 1987, Honda followed the VFR with a racing version, the RC30. While the engine was outwardly similar to the VFR's four-cylinder "V," it introduced some impressive technology, including magnesium castings, titanium connecting rods, and a shim-and-bucket valve adjustment system. Chassis improvements centered around a gorgeous, S-shaped, single-sided swing arm of cast alloy.

Honda sold about three hundred road-going RC30s a year in North America in order to meet the homologation requirements for Fred Merkel's Superbike World Championships in 1988 and 1989. The RC30 was a brilliant motorcycle that, for a short time, was utterly dominant on both the street and track. However, by 1990, the other manufacturers had caught up, and it was clear that as good as it was, it wasn't worth the $15,000 price tag. After all, the Kawasaki ZX-7 was just as fast and sold for $6,500. By Honda's own elevated standards, the RC30 has to be seen as a relative failure.

Back in the early seventies, Yamaha made a 500cc single-cylinder "enduro" motorcycle called the TT500. The Yamaha thumper had the power characteristics of the old British singles, with a more modern, oil-tight motor. Specials builders quickly took notice of the motor, and it found its way into street bikes, too. Yamaha built a street version, the SR500. Briefly, in 1986, Yamaha released a motorcycle powered by a distant cousin of the 500, the SRX 600 Super Single. By 1986, the motor had grown into a "four port" single, with twin exhausts and dual carbs, displacing 595cc.

The motor was not fitted with electric start, relying on a kick starter with an automatic decompressor. Vibration was dealt with by incorporating a gear-driven balance shaft. The engine was shoehorned into a very compact double-cradle frame, with rear-set pegs, clip-on handlebars, and twin shocks. Overall weight was held down to 388 pounds (176kg), although the motorcycle feels even smaller.

The Super Single was a brilliant concept—tractable around town and untouchable on a winding mountain road. Unfortunately, American buyers couldn't appreciate a 600cc sport bike with a top speed of less than 100 miles an hour (161kph). It sold well in Europe, but few came to the United States. As a result, Super Singles are common elsewhere, but hard to find in North America.

The most common critiques of modern sport bikes are that the machines all look the same and that the large plastic fairings lack charisma. In response, specials builders and, later, major manufacturers began creating "naked" bikes. These were unfaired, tube-framed motorcycles that put the visual emphasis back on the engine.

Among naked bikes, the Suzuki Bandit 1200 is a standout. It is a handsome machine with adequate handling and a motor that enables throttle-only wheelies in almost any gear. If the naked-bike movement continues to build momentum, the biggest Bandit will come to be seen as the bike that started it all.

The Yamaha GTS1000 is another motorcycle that future collectors may see as pivotal. This is a big touring machine with an extremely innovative single-sided front suspension design. This "hub center" steering has appeared before, notably on the extraordinary Bimota Tesi, and on Yamaha's own "Morpho" concept bike, but the GTS is the first mass-produced machine with the feature.

Yamaha was initially criticized for introducing this technology on a tourer instead of a flat-out sport bike, but it made a wise choice. By using the GTS1000 as its test bed, Yamaha could study the new suspension on a machine whose handling was not critical. In theory, this suspension setup allows for greatly reduced front-end dive under braking and more consistent suspension behavior under cornering loads. Twenty years from now, if every motorcycle has this front end, an early GTS1000 will have been a prophetic purchase.

Yamaha should have called its 1200cc four-cylinder V-Max the "Mad Max." People who say modern motorcycles lack character are not discussing this particular model. As a potential classic, it meets the first requirement: it is definitely distinctive. The V-Max's over-the-top styling includes a bizarre pair of protuberances on the sides of the fuel tank that are either air intakes or some type of cannon.

On second thought, they must be for air because they point forward, and on a V-Max your enemies are always behind you. The sociopathic engine is capable of accelerating 750 pounds (340.5kg) of metal and meat from 0 to 60 miles per hour (96.5kph) in less than three seconds. While it is tempting to give this idiosyncratic design a vote, it ultimately fails to be either a sport bike or a cruiser. Get one if you want, but save some money for a nice tattoo.

In 1984, Kawasaki introduced the GPZ900R Ninja. This was Kawasaki's first water-cooled production motorcycle and their first four-valve-per-cylinder design. The Ninja's engine was a technological tour de force. It was very compact, measuring only 15 inches

(38cm) across all four cylinders. A balance shaft beneath the crank eliminated secondary imbalances, cutting vibration. This in turn allowed Kawasaki engineers to mount the engine rigidly, which eliminated the need for a cradle frame. With no frame beneath the engine, the motor could be carried slightly lower; thus, the lack of vibration actually improved corner clearance.

The Ninja neatly straddles the historically significant Z1 and Kawasaki's present-day ZX models, which are the best of the current transverse Fours. The early Ninjas are almost certainly destined for classic status. However, they will always be overshadowed by the following year's Suzuki GSX-R 750.

"Where do motorcycles go from here?" That question was asked by veteran technical editor Kevin Cameron in <u>Cycle</u> magazine. The GSX-R completely redefined the high-performance street motorcycle and was without question the most significant new design since the Honda 750 in 1968. It featured an oil-cooled, sixteen-valve motor that sat in a rigid aluminum frame. The total effect was not just one of great acceleration and speed, but equally brilliant handling and braking.

The GSX-R was a motorcycle that needed a racetrack to be fully appreciated, and when it got to the track, it rewrote history there, too. Club racers running production "Gixxers" recorded lap times that, ten years previously, had been the exclusive province of Grand Prix riders on cost-is-no-object works racers.

The introduction of the GSX-R by Suzuki marked the beginning of even more intense competition among the Japanese Big Four. The lead changed hands several times, forcing Suzuki to update the GSX-R in 1988 and again in 1990, but the model still carries its flag, both in the marketplace and in Superbike competition. It is definitely the classic motorcycle of the 1980s, and even ten years later we are still waiting for the answer to Kevin Cameron's question: where, indeed, do motorcycles go from here?

The TD2 and TR3 were replaced by the TZ 250 and 350 in the early seventies. In the early 1970s, all the leading privateers rode these production racers, which were reasonable facsimiles of the ones ridden by Yamaha's factory stars.

first Daytona victory (his dad, Floyd Emde, had given Indian its last). To the dismay of the four-stroke riders, the Yamaha displaced only 350cc, making it the smallest motorcycle ever to win the Daytona 200.

Small, effective racing two-strokes were familiar territory for Yamaha by the early seventies. In 1965, Phil Read won the 250cc world championship on the air-cooled RD56. This was a powerful machine, but Read had to ride with his hand ready at the clutch, for its motor threatened to seize and cause a crash at any second. With macabre humor, Read called the motorcycle "Whispering Death."

At the Japanese Grand Prix, which was the final race of 1965, Hailwood rode to victory on the spectacular Honda Six, and Read told him later

that, once he realized that he couldn't stay with the Honda, he purposely allowed Hailwood to win by a wide margin so that Yamaha would build him an all-new machine. Read was that kind of relentless competitor, and he broached few friendships, even within his Yamaha team.

Yamaha did build Read a water-cooled RD05 for 1966, and Read held up his end of the bargain by winning another championship. Soon after, Yamaha withdrew from Grands Prix and began supplying production racers, which it based on its 250 and 350cc street bikes. The 250 class bike was called a TD2, the 350 a TR3. Yamaha had obviously solved most of the seizure problems by then, as these bikes reverted to air cooling and were still sufficiently reliable to finish first and second in the 1970 250cc championship. This was an incredible result for a production racer, and especially impressive given that it obviously had a lot in common with the street-going YDS2.

Racing results like Emde's victory at Daytona gave Yamaha a real edge in the marketing of brilliant lightweight sports bikes such as the RD350. They cost (and weighed!) much less than four-strokes and easily outmaneuvered bikes like the Mach III. On a winding road, Yamaha's street bikes had few equals, and none at the price. Soon after the release of the seven-port RD, *Motorcyclist* magazine was of the opinion that it "will doubtless come to be considered a classic sporting roadster."

Yamaha continued to develop the line of two-stroke twins well into the eighties. The RZ350 became the clubman's choice over much of the racing world. Its big brother was the radical four-cylinder "V," designated the RZ500, which was one of the first two-stroke Grand Prix–style race replicas.

These interesting two-strokes are rarely seen in the United States, where they fell prey to pollution laws. Instead of building compliant two-stroke engines, most manufacturers simply stopped exporting two-stroke road bikes into the United States. It was a case of "out of sight, out of mind" for American motorcyclists, and two-strokes have made few inroads since, even though modern designs are far less polluting.

Suzuki's entry into the American luxury cruiser market was an interesting two-stroke triple, and it also ended up being thrown out with the bathwater. Or was that coolant? The 1971 Suzuki GT750 was the first mass-produced motorcycle to use water cooling.

Suzuki had carefully positioned the GT750 as a sports touring bike to avoid comparison with the

Ghost Bikes

Collectors value different makes and models of motorcycle according to qualities of engineering, design, and manufacture. But besides makes and models, there are individual machines that, because of their history, become the focus of intense interest. Team Obsolete's MV Augusta 500 is an example of such a motorcycle. It was the last four-stroke to win a Grand Prix, which was simultaneously the last victory for Giacomo Agostini. It embodies a particularly vibrant period in Grand Prix competition.

Of course, few racing motorcycles are retired in original condition. Most are crashed, salvaged, and modified over the course of ongoing development. Forks, chassis, engines, and frames may all be exchanged, making it impossible to confirm or deny that some once-famous bikes even exist at all. Here are a few such "ghost bikes" missing (as far as I know) from the world's collections.

Marlon Brando's Triumph Thunderbird from <u>The Wild One</u> is one of the "most seen" bikes of all time. The movie provided timely publicity for Triumph, and sales of the Thunderbird increased after the film's release. The bike in the film appears stock, with Triumph's "Twinseat" fitted so that Brando could take the film's female star (Mary Murphy) for a ride. Much to the delight of Triumph's marketing department, the ride seemed to liberate Murphy's previously staid libido.

This particular motorcycle's effect on women may have been the reason that it later became the subject of some debate. A few years ago, someone claimed to have this very machine. The Letters column of a specialist magazine featured a series of letters about the claim, some in support and others refuting it. Eventually, someone wrote in to explain that he had been the prop manager on the film, and that Brando's bike had been sold to a California racer, who had subsequently destroyed it in a crash.

Another Hollywood ghost bike is the motorcycle ridden by Steve McQueen in <u>The Great Escape</u>. While it plays a minor role in the film and the famous "jump scene" lasts only seconds, this shot still leaps to mind long after the 1963 film has disappeared, even from late-night television.

McQueen's attempt to jump the fence on a motorcycle captured the public imagination because his real-life riding skills were well publicized. He was a regular racer in the competitive California scrambles scene in the early sixties, and even competed on the American National Team in the International Six Day Trials in 1964. He could have performed the film stunt, but the producers wouldn't let the star risk himself on the shot, so McQueen's racing mentor, Bud Ekins, stood in. Ekins knew that it was out of the question to try it on a real German military bike, and dressed up a 1961 Triumph Trophy with a clunky front fender, luggage racks, and a solo seat. A coat of olive drab paint completed the ruse.

While all this was made up, there was a real motorcycle "great escape," as thrilling as anything imagined by a Hollywood scriptwriter. In 1939, the International Six Day Trials were staged in the hills around Salzburg, only days before the outbreak of World War II.

Britain was represented by a team of Army dispatch riders on Nortons and BSAs. By the fifth day, the political situation was worsening dramatically. The British team realized that completing the event might well leave them trapped behind enemy lines. Germany had issued a call for general mobilization: travel within the country required special permits, roadblocks and military police were everywhere, and virtually all gasoline had been commandeered by the Wehrmacht. Despite these challenges, the British team leaped on their motorcycles and made a successful dash for the Swiss border!

Before the war, Harley-Davidsons were manufactured under license in Japan. Indians were exported to Japan, where they were popular. Soichiro Honda is said to have owned a Scout for many years. Unfortunately for collectors, it is doubtful that Honda's Indian sur-

Above: **Stuntman Bud Ekins knew that real WWII military bikes were too ponderous for *The Great Escape*'s famous jump scene. A 1961 Tiger was used instead.** *Left:* **Motorcycle marketers have long sold machines to men, on the premise that they would have this effect on women.** *Below:* **1952 Indian Chief Roadmaster. Indian sent a similar frame to Vincent, where a Rapide engine was fitted. The project went no further than prototyping.**

vived the war, bombings, and earthquakes that plagued Hamamatsu.

Over the years, Indians have figured in the history of other manufacturers besides Honda. In 1930, Phil Vincent received an Indian engine for the purpose of prototyping an Indian-engined Vincent. In 1947, when Indian was foundering, it sent a Chief chassis to England, where a Vincent Rapide engine was converted to hand shift. This "Vindian" was seen from time to time on the streets of Springfield. Indian employees remember that it was dismantled and salvaged for parts in Indian's last days.

While we would all like to begin our collections with a Brough Superior, Vincent HRD, or Manx Norton, the reality is that such motorcycles, depending on condition, will cost from $10,000 to $100,000. A person with average means and a growing interest in classic motorcycles would be well advised to begin collection with a bike that is not yet coveted by established collectors. Besides saving money, setting one's sights a little lower will get you a bike that's more suited to regular use. Motorcycles are pieces of living history, and as such they are better ridden than hidden.

It is risky, in a book like this, to quote prices. Obviously, condition is everything, and a low-mileage, absolutely original machine is worth many times the price of a well-aged runner. With this proviso, the following bikes are all bona fide classics that are still available (as this book goes to press) for prices from $500 to $2,500.

If you are looking for a bike from before 1965, you must look beyond the glamour motorcycles of the period. The best of the British, European, and American iron has all been collected for some time now. However, the utility bikes of the period were built in larger numbers and still make stylish runabouts. The 1950s Vespas benefit from low prices and an established "cult" that makes sourcing parts and information easy. From the early 1960s, the French Velosolex is the perfect thing to ride to the store for some bread.

While the key motorcycles are now recognized by most collectors, prices are still modest for many Japanese invasion bikes from the mid-sixties. The Yamaha YDS3 Big Bear, the Suzuki T10 Super Six, or a Honda Dream are full of memories for older baby boomers. From the late sixties, unit construction Triumphs are still eminently rideable, and the support networks that classic bike enthusiasts rely on are especially well established for the British marques.

Above: **This "Mod" Vespa would have been right at home on Carnaby Street in 1960s London.** *Below:* **1965 Yamaha YDS2 "Big Bear." These two-strokes were rugged, affordable, and surprisingly quick. The YDS2 bears a strong family resemblance to Yamaha's air-cooled factory racers of the mid-sixties, and is the clear ancestor of the "RD" series of sports bikes Yamaha introduced in the 1970s.**

Lots of Honda Fours have survived from the early seventies. The smaller ones, like the 500 Four and the CB400, are just starting to attract the attention they deserve. They outhandle their big brother.

BMW/5s from this era are great buys. They have the traits one expects in a true classic—timeless design and fabulous build quality—and they're mechanic-friendly, too.

Moving into the mid-seventies, prices of the Kawasaki Z1 still do not reflect its significance. The same is true for the GL1000 Gold Wing. Twenty years from now, any of these motorcycles could have the sort of status that an Ariel Square Four or a Harley Knucklehead has today.

That said, one of the best things about collecting classic motorcycles is that each person's unique memories and experiences give him his own favorites. Growing up in Switzerland, I was able to ride a moped at age fourteen. I had a Puch Condor; I can't imagine what property of the machine inspired such a lofty name. What I aspired to, however, was a Kreidler Florette. This was also a 50cc. I was realistic about what I could afford and my parents would allow. Compared to my Puch, these tiny German creations were real motorcycles. People actually raced them.

Soon after my family moved to Canada, I switched to a Kawasaki scrambler. Kreidler motorcycles didn't cross my mind again until I walked into the Reynolds-Alberta Museum while researching this book. There was a Florette, exactly as I remembered after twenty-five years. It triggered a flood of memories. What was just another motorbike to most museum visitors was my dream machine.

Kawasaki Mach IV, which was a bigger, even faster version of the Mach III. American riders were bemused at best (they nicknamed the Suzuki the "Water Buffalo"), but it stands as one of the more interesting attempts to stretch the boundaries of the touring class. If modern research into "direct injection" engines spawns a new line of fuel-efficient, low-pollution, two-stroke cruisers, they will owe much to the GT750.

In 1939, the Triumph Speed Twin had seemed like the first modern motorcycle. Thirty years later, the Bonneville still carried the flag for Turner's aesthetic master stroke. Over the years, Bonnevilles had been the subject of slow—all right, very slow—improvement. They got a stiffer chas-

Above and right: **After the dark days under management by AMF, Harley-Davidson managers bought the company back. The introduction of the "Evolution" engine marked a return to quality-control levels which had not been seen in Harleys since the early 1940s.**

sis and unit construction of engine and gearbox in the sixties. Cam lobe wear problems were finally addressed, with the addition of a simple oilway. In 1971, an all-new frame was designed, with an integral oil tank in the large-diameter backbone tube. Responding to pressure from American dealers and legislators, the last Bonnevilles were bored out to 750cc, and the gearshift was relocated to the left side of the engine.

Meanwhile, the BSA group entered the decade with a staggering financial loss. In a series of deals

between financiers and the British government, the entire remaining British motorcycle industry was finally reduced to one company: Norton-Villiers-Triumph. It was apparent that Triumph's Meriden plant, where the Bonneville was manufactured, should be closed and its production moved to the much larger BSA facility at Small Heath.

Early Superbikes

Ironically, the Meriden staff was optimistic about the potential of the new Bonneville, but now faced the loss of their jobs. In desperation, they blockaded the factory. The British Midlands are union country, and the tactic, after much tortured negotiation, led to the formation of a workers' cooperative that continued to produce excellent Bonnevilles. There was no money available for further development, and through the early seventies there were stretches when Triumph shipments ground to a complete halt. Triumph dealers went bankrupt or signed distribution agreements with other brands.

Norton-Villiers-Triumph ceased production in 1978. The Meriden factory was sold to make way for a housing development in the early eighties. Triumph production continued, albeit on a reduced scale, in Coventry, where the company had been founded eighty years before. Where there were once two hundred British marques, Triumph alone has survived. The new line of Japanese-influenced, retro-style sports tourers share only a logo with Triumph's past.

The best Bonnevilles of all are perhaps those of 1968–1970. Rubber mounting of the oil tanks cured a chronic cracking problem. (The final oil-in-frame design, inspired by the Trackmaster dirt-track racing frames, is scorned by traditionalists and raises seats too high.) Automatic spark advance, which had arrived with unit construction, makes them easier to start and more tractable at idling speeds. The engine, not yet bored to 750cc, was a little more durable, and they finally stopped leaking (as much) oil.

Ten years earlier, these would have been awe-inspiring motorcycles. Employees on the shop floor in Meriden did know, way back then, what the Bonnie needed, but Triumph's upper-class management never deigned to listen to the working-class people who actually built the bikes. For years, Triumph boss Edward Turner was chauffeured to work in a Daimler limousine.

Still, even thirty years after the Speed Twin, there was no denying Turner's genius for design as well as engineering. His were the first mass-produced motorcycles to leave behind the aesthetics of the "Machine Age." By building internal oilways instead of external oil lines and by streamlining the engine castings, the Speed Twin embraces the future. The Bonneville was heir to this aesthetic and even at the end of its model life was a most handsome motorcycle.

In 1969, the American Machine and Foundry Company (AMF) purchased control of Harley-Davidson. Through the early seventies, motorcycle sales were artificially buoyed by rising fuel prices. AMF seemed to be on a roll, raising sales volumes from less than thirty thousand units per year to about sixty thousand in 1975.

The price of this increased production, however, was a catastrophic decrease in the quality of machines Harley was putting out. Frustrated

Early Superbikes

Above: **The Kawasaki KZ 650 was introduced in 1977.** *Opposite, top:* **1970 Triumph Bonneville.** *Opposite, bottom:* **Suzuki Intruder. As Harley-Davidson prices rose in the 1980s, every Japanese manufacturer introduced bald-faced copies of big, V-twin cruisers. While these fakes worked fine and cost far less than genuine American iron, they have, if anything, only increased Harley-Davidson's pose value.**

Harley-Davidson dealers were being forced to rebuild engines still under warranty, often after only a few thousand miles. Used Harleys were described as "pre-AMF" in classified ads.

Harley-Davidson was already in a weakened state in 1975 when Honda, for the first time, exported a motorcycle aimed directly at Harley's market. The motorcycle it sent was the 1,000cc Gold Wing, and in typical Honda fashion, it completely redefined its class.

People were momentarily taken aback at their first glimpse of the Gold Wing. If anything, it seemed even more massive than its reported weight of more than 600 pounds (272.5kg). Bill Haylock, editor of the British magazine *Bike*, criticized its size and handling, and took further offense at Honda's blatant efforts to redefine and sanitize "biking." His vitriolic attack on the Gold Wing caused Honda to pull its advertising from *Bike*, and it was years before the magazine was provided with its next Honda test machine.

Perhaps because of such mixed reviews, Honda's first year sales of the Wing were only about 10 percent of their forecast. On American highways, however, the proof was in the riding. The Honda development team, led by engineer Toshio Nozue, had taken pains to keep the weight low. The water-cooled flat four layout helped from the start, and the gearbox was actually below the driveshaft. The real gas tank is under the seat, while the dummy tank folds open to reveal electrics, tools, radiator overflow, and storage. The unnerving torque effects of the shaft drive were minimized by cleverly setting up the large alternator to

Above: **1975 Honda Gold Wing. Gold Wings were sold with spoked wheels for only two years. Early GL1000 models such as this one are already recognized as classics.** *Right:* **1977 AMF Harley-Davidson Super Glide, on duty in West Palm Beach. In the late 1970s, the big Harleys were plagued with quality control problems. Police contracts, which often still specified "American made," were one of the last areas where AMF could effectively market them.**

spin in the opposite direction. All things considered, it was surprisingly manageable, and word-of-mouth advertising among American riders quickly built support for Honda's magnum opus.

On the highway, the engine was almost completely silent, and there was no vibration at all. It would pull from jogging speed to interstate speed in any gear from second to fifth. In terms of straight line performance, no Harley-Davidson or BMW could touch it, and even the BMW (to say nothing of the Harley) bowed to the Gold Wing's ruggedness.

Initially, Gold Wings were sold stripped. But a new generation of highway cruisers realized that

the machine could be loaded up with fairing, saddlebags, passengers, and even trailers without straining the superb engine. These "dressed" bikes had been the most profitable part of Harley-Davidson's market, and Harley sales slumped through the late seventies. By 1980, AMF was ready to admit defeat, and it seemed Harley-Davidson's end was in sight. In a last-ditch effort that showed confidence in the once-mighty brand, a group of Harley-Davidson executives purchased the motorcycle division from AMF.

By emphasizing AMF's quality-control failures, Honda and the Gold Wing helped trigger Harley-Davidson's management buyout. The subsequent turnaround of Harley-Davidson is a modern legend in American business. Riding into the second century of motorcycling, Harley-Davidson's status as the world's longest continuously operating motorcycle company seems secure.

Early Superbikes

Bibliography

Ayrton, C.J. *The Hamlyn Guide to Japanese Motorcycles.* London: Hamlyn Publishing Group, 1982.

Bacon, Roy. *Ariel: The Postwar Models.* London: Osprey, 1983.

Bacon, Roy. *BSA Twins and Triples.* London: Osprey, 1980.

Bacon, Roy. *The Illustrated Triumph Motorcycles Buyer's Guide.* Isle of Wight, England: Niton Publishing, 1993.

Birkitt, Malcolm. *Honda Gold Wing.* London: Osprey, 1995.

Brooke, A. Lindsay, and David Gaylin. *Triumph Motorcycles in America.* Osceola, WI: Motorbooks International, 1993.

Burns, Rod. *Velocette: A Development History of the MSS, Venom, Viper, Thruxton, and Scrambler Models.* Newbury Park, CA: Haynes, 1982.

Croucher, Robert. *The Story of BMW Motorcycles.* Sparkford, UK: Patrick Stephens, 1982.

Currie, Bob. *Great British Motorcycles of the Fifties.* Sussex, UK: Temple Press.

Davies, Ivor. *Triumph Thunderbird.* Newbury Park, CA: Haynes, 1984.

Emde, Don. *The Daytona 200.* Laguna Niguel, CA: Motorcycle Heritage Press/Infosport, 1990.

Girdler, Allan. *The Illustrated Harley Davidson Buyer's Guide.* Osceola, WI: Motorbooks International, 1986.

Hailwood, Mike, and Walker Murray. *The Art of Motorcycle Racing.* London: Cassell, 1963.

Harper, Roy. *The Vincent H.R.D. Story.* Sussex, UK: Vincent Publishing Company, 1975.

Hatfield, Jerry. *American Racing Motorcycles.* Newbury Park, CA: Haynes, 1982.

Hatfield, Jerry. *Illustrated Indian Motorcycle Buyer's Guide.* Osceola, WI: Motorbooks International, 1989.

Johnstone, Gary. *Classic Motorcycles.* London: Boxtree, 1993.

Knittel, Stefan, and Roland Slabon. *The Illustrated BMW Motorcycle Buyer's Guide.* Osceola, WI: Motorbooks International, 1990.

Louis, Harry, and Bob Currie. *The Story of Triumph Motorcycles.* Sparkford, UK: Patrick Stephens, 1975.

Main-Smith, Bruce. *The Gold Star Book.* Great Britain: Bruce Main-Smith Retail Ltd., 1974.

Magrath, Derek. *Norton, The Complete Story.* Marlborough, Wiltshire: Crowood Press, 1991.

Nicholson, J.B. *Modern Motorcycle Mechanics.* Saskatoon, SK: Nicholson Brothers Motorcycles, Ltd., 1974.

Norris, Martin. *Rolling Thunder.* Philadelphia: Courage Books, 1992.

Sucher, Harry V. *Inside American Motorcycling And The American Motorcycle Association 1900-1910.* Laguna Niguel, CA: Infosport, 1995

Sucher, Harry. *The Iron Redskin.* Newbury Park, CA: Haynes, 1977.

Tragatsch, Erwin. *The Complete Illustrated Encyclopedia of the World's Motorcycles.* New York: Holt Rinehart and Winston, 1977.

Warring, R.H. *The Book of the NSU Quickly.* London: Pitman Publishing, 1971.

Wiesner, Wolfgang. *Harley Davidson Photographic History.* Osceola, WI: Motorbooks International, 1989.

Willoughby, Vic. *Classic Motorcycles.* Sussex, UK: Temple Press, 1982.

Wilson, Hugo. *The Ultimate Motorcycle Book.* Toronto: HarperCollins, 1993.

Wright, David K. *The Harley Davidson Motor Company: An Official Ninety Year History.* Osceola, WI: Motorbooks International, 1993.

Index

Index

Ghost bikes, 109
Gilera, 55, *55*, 60–61, 70
Gold Star, BSA, 59–60, *60*, 83
Gold Wing, Honda, 110, 113–114, *114*
Goulding sidecar, 49
The Great Escape, 109
GSX-R 750, Suzuki, 107
GT750, Suzuki, 108, 111
GTS1000, Yamaha, 107
Guzzi. *See* Moto Guzzi

H

Haas, Walter, 74
Hailwood, Mike, 46, 58, 68, 85, *85*, *93*,
      96, *96*, 108
Hamamatsu Technical School, 84
Harley, William, 36, 37
Harley, William J., 77
Harley-Davidson, 20, 30–33, 35–37, 43, *43*,
      46, 56–57, 76–77, 98, 112–113, 114
   Army issue, *61*
   chopper, *75*
   Depression and, 18, 34–35
   Evolution engine, 106, 111, *111*
   lightweight market and, 87–89
Haylock, Bill, 113
Hedstrom, Oscar, 17
Hell's Angels, 56, *57. See also* Gangs,
      outlaw
Helvetia, 72
Hendee, George W., 17, 27
Hendee Special, Indian, 23
Henderson, Bill, 18, 27, 36
Henne, Ernst, 72
Hildebrand and Wolfmuller, 16, *16*
Hillclimbing, *30*, 82
Hoffman, 73
Hollous, Rupert, 84
Honda, 80–81, 84–85, *85*, 89, 94–97,
      106–107, 110, 113–114
Honda, Soichiro, 74, *84*, 84–85, 109
Hopwood, Bert, 58, 93
Hummer, Harley-Davidson, 46
Humper, Kawasaki, 107
Hydra-Glide, Harley-Davidson, 56, *56*

I

Imola, Ducati, 103, 104
Indian Sales Company, 17, *17*, 20, 23, 27,
      28–29, 30, 36, 37, *38*, *40–41*, 45,
      48, 49, *49*, *71*, *109*
   Depression and, 18, 34

in Japan, 109
   Model H, 22–23
   trademark, 50, *50*
Innocenti, 63–64
Interceptor, Honda, 106
International, Norton, *54*
Intruder, Suzuki, *112*
Investing in classics, 106–107
Isetta three-wheeler, 76
Isolastic frame, 93
Iver-Johnson, 19

J

James, 47
JD series, Harley-Davidson, *30–31*, 32–33
JH, Harley-Davidson, 30–31
Johnson Motors, 83, 86
Jubilee, Norton, *82*

K

K100, BMW, 106
Kaaden, Walter, 46
Kawasaki, *90–91*, 92, 97, *97*, 102–103,
      103, 106, *106*, 107, 110, *113*
KH, Harley-Davidson, *54*
Kitagawa Motorcycle Company, 85
Knucklehead, Harley-Davidson, *35*, 35–36, *49*
Kompressor, BMW, 37, 76
KR, Harley-Davidson, 98
Kuchen, Richard, 73
KZ650, Kawasaki, *113*

L

Lambretta, *62*, 63–64, 64
Lawrence, T.E., 27
Le Mans, Moto Guzzi, *104*
Leader, Ariel, *81*, 81–82, 82
Liberati, Libero, 63, *63*
Lightening, Buell, *107*
Lomas, Bill, 70
Luchinelli, Marco, 106

M

Mach III, Kawasaki, 97
Manganese Bronze Holdings, 92
Mann, Dick, 83, *83*
Manx, Norton, 47, 55, *55*, 58
Marketing, *109*
Marusho, 73
Marvin, Lee, 56

Masetti, Umberto, 63
Matchless, 26, 47, *47*, 83
Maybach, Wilhelm, 16
Mazza, Ruggero, 69–70
McCandless brothers, 55
McCullen, Archie, 19
McQueen, Steve, 109
Meguro, 97
Meier, Walter, 76
Menos, 72
Merkel, 20
   Flying, 19, *20*
Miller, Sammy, 82
Minter, Derek, 46
Molloy, Ginger, 97
Moore, Walter, 74
Mopeds, 51
Moto Guzzi, 44, 63, 70, *104*
Motosacoche a Geneve, 20
MV Agusta, 63, *68*, 68–70, 96, 104, 109
MV (Meccanica Verghere), 68
MZ (Motorradweke Zschopan), 46, *46*, 72

N

Naked bikes, 107
Neracar scooter, 19
Nerachar, J., 19
New York Streak, Kawasaki, 102
Ninja, Kawasaki, 106, 107
Nixon, Gary, 57
Norton, *31*, 31–32, 42–43, *43*, 47, *54*,
      55, *55*, 57–58, *58*, *82*, 97
Norton-Villiers, 92–94
Norton-Villiers-Triumph, 111
Nozue, Toshio, 113
NSU, 64, 74–75, 84

O

On Any Sunday, 87

P

Page, Val, 82
Panther, Phelon and Moore, 48
Pasolini, Renzo, 89
Petrali, Joe, 37, *37*
Phelon and Moore, 48
Phillis, Tom, *85*, 96
Piaggio, 63
Pixie, Ariel, 82
Police fleets, *71*, 77, *95*, 97, *114–115*
Porcupine, AJS, 45

Index

119

Photography Credits

Courtesy American Honda: pp. 80 top, 84 both, 85 all

Automobile Quarterly: pp. 2, 10, 14-15, 20 bottom, 21, 26 top left, 30 top, 32, 45, 54 top, 92 bottom, 99, 114-115

Classic Bike: pp. 46 top, 64 left, 74, 83 right, 89

Corbis-Bettmann: pp. 18 top, 26 top right, 36 left, 109 bottom left

©Kathryn Culley: pp. 48 top right, 68 top, 110 top, 111 bottom, 112 bottom, 113

©Mark Gardiner: pp. 102 top, 105

©Jerry Heasley: p. 49

Courtesy Kawasaki Motors: p. 106 center

Kobal Collection: pp. 56 top, 109 top

©Andrew Morland: back endpaper; all sidebar backgrounds; pp. 16 bottom, 20 top, 22 bottom, 27, 28-29, 31 top, 34 both, 35 both, 38-39, 43 both, 44 bottom, 47, 54 bottom, 55 top, 56 bottom, 57 top, 61, 63 bottom, 64-65, 66-67, 68 bottom, 70 center, 73, 77 both, 81, 86, 87, 92 top, 93 both, 94, 95, 96 all, 103, 107

Motorcycle Heritage Museum: pp. 72, 97 top, 110 bottom, 114

©The National Motor Museum, Beaulieu, England: front endpaper; pp. 5, 6, 16 top, 17 both, 19, 24-25, 26 bottom, 31 bottom, 33, 40-41, 42 top, 44 top, 46 bottom, 48 top left, 55 bottom, 59, 62, 76, 82 top, 106 right, 108, 109 bottom right

National Motorcycle Museum: p. 71

©John Owens 1997: pp. 78-79

Quadrant Picture Library: pp. 7, 8, 11, 12, 38 left, 42 bottom, 50-51, 52-53, 57 bottom, 58, 60, 70 top, 75, 82 bottom, 90-91, 100-101, 102 bottom, 104 both, 106 left, 111 top, 112 top

©Team Obsolete/Maurice Bula 1996: p. 69 top

Underwood & Underwood/Corbis-Bettmann: pp. 23, 48 bottom

UPI/Corbis-Bettmann: pp. 18 bottom, 22 top, 30 bottom, 36 right, 37 both, 44 left, 57 center, 63 top, 69 bottom, 83 left, 97 bottom

©Troyce Walls: p. 88